SEEING
the
HEART
of
CHRIST

SEEING

the

HEART

of

CHRIST

How Jesus Cares
for Hurting People

Bill Crowder

Seeing the Heart of Christ: How Jesus Cares for Hurting People

© 2018 by Bill Crowder

All rights reserved.

Discovery House is affiliated with Our Daily Bread Ministries, Grand Rapids, Michigan.

Requests for permission to quote from this book should be directed to: Permissions Department, Discovery House, PO Box 3566, Grand Rapids, MI 49501, or contact us by email at permissionsdept@dhp.org.

All Scripture quotations, unless otherwise indicated, are from the New American Standard Bible®, copyright © 1960, 1962, 1963, 1968, 1971, 1972, 1973, 1975, 1977, 1995 by The Lockman Foundation. Used by permission. www.lockman.org.

Interior design by Nicholas Richardson

ISBN: 978-1-62707-673-9

Library of Congress Cataloging-in-Publication Data
Names: Crowder, Bill, author.
Title: Seeing the heart of Christ : how Jesus cares for hurting people / Bill
    Crowder.
Description: Grand Rapids : Discovery House, 2018.
Identifiers: LCCN 2017056150 | ISBN 9781627076739 (pbk.)
Subjects: LCSH: Jesus Christ–Friends and associates. | Caring–Religious
    aspects–Christianity. | Healing–Religious aspects–Christianity.
Classification: LCC BT590.F7 C76 2018 | DDC 232.9/5--dc23
LC record available at https://lccn.loc.gov/2017056150

Printed in the United States of America

Second printing in 2018

*For
Marlene.
Thanks.
I love you.*

Contents

Acknowledgments

I am primarily a Bible teacher, but I have also been blessed with the opportunity and privilege of writing. Because I feel that writing is not my stronger area of giftedness when compared with preaching, I am grateful for the people who help me capture ideas that I feel are significant and assist me in presenting them to you in, hopefully, a meaningful and compelling way.

I have a terrific team that helps form ideas, shape language, and present the stories of the Gospels in a way that will, I trust, enrich your understanding of and appreciation for the Christ who came to us and for us.

I am speaking of the folks at Discovery House who have been so supportive of me. My deep gratitude goes to Ken Petersen, our publisher, and his terrific team of Miranda Gardner, Andy Rogers, Dave Branon, and more. I deeply appreciate each person who has helped this project on its way.

As grateful as I am for the team at DH, I am even more grateful for the team I have at home. My wife, Marlene, has been my partner in life and ministry for some forty years and continues to be my best friend. Our kids and their families have grown much since I began the writing portion of my ministry, and I am grateful for each of them and the little ones that have come along as well. Our family has been a great source of joy and blessing, for which I am thankful.

And to you, the reader, it is my deep desire that your own journey with Jesus will find new depth as you explore these encounters. Seeing Him respond so fully to men and women like you and me is beyond imagination. My desire is that the heart of Jesus can become the most real thing in our lives as we learn His heart together. Thanks for reading.

Perspective

It was such a simple, surprising question that I never saw it coming. Scot McKnight, in his book *The King Jesus Gospel*, asked a basic question about the first four books of the New Testament: "Why do we call them *gospels*?" I had to pause, because I had never given this question a moment's thought.

They just *are*, I had always believed. But for someone living in a culture where we equate the word *gospel* with the plan of salvation, it became an intriguing question. I gave serious consideration to McKnight's question: What makes these four books "good news," which is the actual meaning of the word *gospel*?

In one sense, these four records *are* good news because they culminate the story of the Old Testament—fulfilling the promise of the cross and the resurrection found in the Bible's first thirty-nine books. The anticipation of a rescuer and the longing for Messiah propelled the ancient people of God through centuries marked by failure and captivity—followed by a periodic turning to God, which was a revival that reminded them of their foundational moorings.

In another sense, the four Gospels are good news because they record for us the story of the greatest life ever lived. But make no mistake. These are not just biographies—although they do tell us the necessary details of Jesus's life. The books of Matthew, Mark, Luke, and John are also witnesses to us—telling us that the Word

(Jesus) had become flesh and had lived among us (John 1:14) to bear our griefs, carry our sorrows, and forgive our failings.

Most of all, however, we see in the Gospels the true story of Jesus as He lived out His mission to reveal the Father to us. In John 1, as the beloved apostle explores with us the mysteries of the incarnation, he makes a decisive statement about the *why* behind Jesus's coming. He wrote: "No one has seen God at any time. The only begotten Son, who is in the bosom of the Father, He has declared Him" (John 1:18 NKJV).

John's point is profound! Jesus came to do for us what we needed the most. He came to explain to us the Father, who seemed distant and inaccessible. He came to show us the Father, whose love for the world could only be satisfied by offering His Son as payment for our sin and brokenness. He was the God who imprinted himself on the heart of every human (Romans 1:18–20) but with whom we could not have fellowship without the sacrifice of His Son—who came to live in human flesh in the middle of human circumstances and human heartaches. Jesus has declared to us the heart of the Father by showing that heart—a mission revealed in John 1:18 and proclaimed to be completed in John 14:9 when Jesus said, "He who has seen Me has seen the Father."

What did the people who lived alongside Jesus see? And how did they see what they observed in Him?

A partial answer, at least, is found in the episodes we will explore together in this book. As we observe Jesus interacting with the hurting people of His day, we see that He is not just relieving the pains and struggles of men and women engaged in a life that was too big for them. As vital as that is, we also see in every case something of the Father that Jesus is declaring. Something of the "Abba" (see Romans 8:15) who adopted followers of Christ into His family then and who still today gives us the capability of being called sons and daughters of God. It is my desire that we not only marvel at the work of the God-man Jesus but that we also learn about the heart of the Father that Christ revealed as He interacted with people in need.

Jesus's heart for hurting people is a reflection of the heart of the Father. And that is really good news!

A Heart That Touches
Jesus and a Leper

As a boy, I reveled in the adventures of Eliot Ness and his intrepid G-men as I watched Robert Stack portray the legendary crime-fighter on the television show *The Untouchables*. Blazing across our TV screen in glorious black-and-white, Ness and his team of United States Treasury agents battled corruption, crime, and the mob.

Perhaps the key word there is *corruption*. One of the greatest challenges these law officers faced while operating in prohibition-era Chicago was that a significant number of the city's officials, judges, and police were in the mob's pocket. Through bribes and threats, the criminal elements controlled the city so thoroughly that any serious investigation of their activity was virtually impossible.

Into that mess came a small group of difference-makers who were called "untouchables" because they operated above pay-offs. They refused to be drawn into the mire of the city's dark underbelly, they were unmoved by the lure of money, and they refused to shrink before threat. They were beyond the reach of the city's criminal element. They were *untouchable.*

About the same time as I was watching *The Untouchables*, I learned in school that there were cultures in the world that practiced the social stratification of caste systems. Caste systems layer society into specific groups based on the family's status when a child is born. It considers roles in society as hereditary and static, with no hope for moving up any kind of social strata. By dividing the population into these hardened categories, this system created its own set of *untouchables*—people who inhabit the lowest rung of society's ladder. They are off-limits because they were considered "less-than," meaning they are insignificant or even non-persons who do not fit into the important castes that are looked to carry the weight of society's expectations.

Years later, I came to understand that in the days of Jesus, Israel had its own set of untouchables. These were not categorized metaphorically, however. Their untouchability was not the result of moral resilience or social labeling. They were literally untouchable because they carried a disease that bore deep spiritual and physical implications. They were lepers.

In first-century Israel, lepers were the embodiment of everything that was bad in the human condition. Marked by a disease that screamed of heartache, despair, and brokenness, lepers were outcasts—and it was not simply because of the physical realities of the disease. Leprosy also carried intense spiritual implications. And as we will see, the crushing loneliness resulting from those implications had even been mapped out in the law of Moses.

An Isolating Condition

In the time of Christ, leprosy was not uncommon in the land of Israel—as evidenced by the number of lepers Jesus encountered in His ministry. Leprosy was a living death—the slow dissolution of a body as it decayed away. Dr. Paul Brand (1914–2003), who spent his adult life studying the disease and serving those who suffered with it, said that leprosy destroyed the nerve endings, and as a result physical pain couldn't be felt. This meant that appendages would be literally rubbed off and worn away because there was no sense of restraint (a powerful picture of sin).

In the first century, however, none of this was known. The medical realities of this disease were secondary to its spiritual overtones. In a land where ceremonial purity was necessary for access to the temple and the sacrificial system, leprosy was a painful path to ceremonial impurity. There were sixty-one ceremonial defilements listed in the Jewish law—restrictions that would cause a person to be disqualified for a time from participating in temple or synagogue life. And of these sixty-one defilements, only touching a dead body was worse than touching a leper.

Even more, the Jews of Jesus's day referred to leprosy as "the finger of God," believing it to be direct punishment from Him. Therefore, only God could cure it. This understanding may have emerged from the ancient story of Moses's sister, Miriam. In Numbers 12, we read that Miriam and Aaron (their brother) spoke out against Moses, undermining his leadership of the Israelites. Apparently, Miriam led in this rebellion, because God disciplined her with leprosy—a severe discipline indeed. She was driven from the community and forced to live in isolation outside the camp. Seven days later, God lifted that punishment, and she was reunited with family and friends. Leprosy was inflicted and leprosy was removed: The finger of God.

The isolation Miriam experienced, however, was the life path for all lepers. In Jewish ceremonial law, this isolation was prescribed for the leper:

> When a man or a woman has bright spots on the skin of the body, even white bright spots, then the priest shall look, and if the bright spots on the skin of their bodies are a faint white, it is eczema that has broken out on the

skin; he is clean. Now if a man loses the hair of his head, he is bald; he is clean. If his head becomes bald at the front and sides, he is bald on the forehead; he is clean. But if on the bald head or the bald forehead, there occurs a reddish-white infection, it is leprosy breaking out on his bald head or on his bald forehead. Then the priest shall look at him; and if the swelling of the infection is reddish-white on his bald head or on his bald forehead, like the appearance of leprosy in the skin of the body, he is a leprous man, he is unclean. The priest shall surely pronounce him unclean; his infection is on his head. As for the leper who has the infection, his clothes shall be torn, and the hair of his head shall be uncovered, and he shall cover his mustache and cry, "Unclean! Unclean!" He shall remain unclean all the days during which he has the infection; he is unclean. He shall live alone; his dwelling shall be outside the camp. (Leviticus 13:38–46)

Notice what was called for in these words. In most life situations, when a person would see that he or she had the symptoms of some kind of illness, the first logical response would be to go to seek medical help—whether it would be seeking out a doctor or in some cultures using traditional healing through herbs or other natural medicines. But because of the spiritual implications of leprosy, the symptoms (dry, crusty patches of skin) required ancient Israelites to go to the priest, not the doctor. The priest would diagnose the problem, and if it was determined to be leprosy, that man or woman's job, family, place in the synagogue, and access to the community would all be taken away. Additionally, the leper's social and spiritual stigma was intensified because he or she was forced to announce the uncleanness to any "clean" individuals encountered along the way.

The horror of a disease that was seen as a walking death sentence was compounded by the knowledge that the person would endure that fate alone. The condition was intensified by solitary confinement. Leprosy conspired to create "untouchables" who were to be put away and never touched. This reality is interjected into a strategic moment in Jesus's fledgling ministry—and the timing is critical. We read about this in Mark 1:40–45.

A Moment of Desperation
"And a leper came to Jesus." (Mark 1:40)

In recent years, a phenomenon known as Black Friday has become something of a national obsession in the United States. On the day after Thanksgiving, stores offer huge discounts on everything from cars to flat-screen TVs to kitchen appliances. As a result, people line up in the wee hours of the morning, sometimes even sleeping in tents on sidewalks overnight, waiting to get the early bird specials on things that they either desperately want for themselves or want to give to someone else for Christmas. This desperate search for bargains often leads to some strange situations—escalating from loud disagreements over who was ahead in line to fistfights over who gets the last super-duper-mega-low-priced giant whatever. Such events have even produced near-riots in which people have been trampled by the pressing mob. These moments of unnecessary desperation have caused tragic consequences.

By contrast, consider a different kind of desperation—the truly necessary urgency of a leper who was aware of the prohibitions of Israel's ceremonial law. Notice again what Leviticus 13:45–46 tells us:

As for the leper who has the infection, his clothes shall be torn, and the hair of his head shall be uncovered, and he shall cover his mustache and cry, "Unclean! Unclean!" He shall remain unclean all the days during which he has the infection; he is unclean. He shall live alone; his dwelling shall be outside the camp.

Now notice the actions of the leper who "came to Jesus" (Mark 1:40). Jesus is coming down from the mountainside (Matthew 8:1) after delivering the Sermon on the Mount, and as always "large crowds followed Him" (8:1). The leper arrives with a heart filled with desperation. Luke, the gospel-writing physician, gives us the impetus behind this man's anxiety, saying that he was "covered with leprosy" (5:12), perhaps indicating that the disease had ravaged his body so extensively that it was in its final stages.

This leper's inevitable appointment with death was approaching, yet the law required him to remain apart from people. To suffer alone. To die in isolation. He refuses, and instead:

- He comes among people, in violation of Moses's law and societal taboos.
- He comes with nothing to lose—in the final stages of the disease.
- He comes after years of being isolated and alone.
- He comes directly to Jesus in the midst of the crowd, and he begs for mercy (Luke 5:12).

As I picture the scene, I see the leper arriving, which is probably a terrifying moment for those following Jesus. At the sight and no doubt the smell of the dying leper, the crowd surely recoiled. Perhaps the man—in desperation to get to Jesus—had not even shouted the required words of warning. It appears that this leper openly violated Mosaic law because his misery has driven him to Jesus.

Yet this man comes to Jesus not only out of desperation but he also comes to Him with a measure of faith: "And a leper came to Jesus, beseeching Him and falling on his knees before Him, and saying, 'If You are willing, You can make me clean'" (Mark 1:40).

This is astonishing! Remember that this is at the very outset of Jesus's public ministry. In Mark's account, Jesus has rescued a demon-possessed man (Mark 1:23–27) and healed Simon Peter's mother-in-law (1:30–31), followed by a season of general healings and deliverances. But it is still the early days of Jesus's public works. This leper—an untouchable outcast—has apparently heard amazing stories about this Nazarene wonder-worker and has connected the dots. When he comes to Jesus, he does so begging for the Teacher's intervention. He falls before Him in an attitude of pleading that pictures worship.

It is an amazing scene made all the more remarkable by the man's words, "If You are willing, You can make me clean" (Mark 1:40). Remember, this man was part of a culture that viewed leprosy as "the finger of God." Leprosy was given by God and could only be removed by God—and this man declares his confidence that Jesus could do what only God can do: Jesus could take away leprosy.

A Kingdom Ethic

As we explore the Gospels, we discover that each gospel record is written to a specific target audience and that each writer is presenting a specific theme about Jesus. Additionally, each of the Gospels has distinct, unique characteristics that help us understand how the writer is telling the story of Jesus.

Why is this important? Here's an example. Although we are looking at this encounter from Mark's Gospel, we must recognize that where it is placed in Matthew's Gospel is significant. Scholars believe that among the Gospel writers Matthew seems to be the one most concerned about the actual chronology of the events. So where does Matthew place this event? He includes it in Matthew 8, which tells us that the event occurred directly after Jesus delivered the Sermon on the Mount.

In that message, Jesus was doing more than just giving one of His major public addresses. He was outlining the ethic of the upside-down kingdom of which He is the King. He was describing a kingdom where the King is a servant and the marginalized are welcome. It is a kingdom where loving and serving take priority over ruling and controlling. This is a message that is much easier to proclaim than it is to live.

After some forty years of having a public teaching ministry, I can affirm that preaching the Scriptures is infinitely easier than living them. Phrases like "practice what you preach" and "don't just talk the talk, walk the walk" underline the challenge before us, as do the words of the apostle James, "Prove yourselves doers of the word, and not merely hearers who delude themselves" (1:22).

So the question is this: Having declared the lofty, noble heart of a better kingdom, would Jesus live out that heart? Would He practice what He preached? We find the answer in Mark 1:41–42.

A Healing Touch

Compassion International is an organization committed to the welfare of children in developing countries. The vision of Compassion perfectly reflects its name—that people in the developed world would have compassion on children in need and respond with a commitment to help meet the needs of those children in developing countries.

Why does it work? Because of the idea of the word *compassion*. *Compassion* is a rich word that challenges us to feel a true concern for another person in pain or in need. In fact, one online dictionary defines *compassion* as "the act or capacity for sharing the painful feelings of another." Compassion goes beyond mere pity or concern—it enters into a person's pain and feels it with him or her.

It should come as no surprise to us that as Jesus walked on the earth He encountered the human condition with a heart of compassion. That was part of His prophesied mission. The ancient sage Isaiah declared of the coming Messiah, "Surely our griefs He Himself bore, and our sorrows He carried" (Isaiah 53:4). Jesus did not come to be a distant observer or a bemused spectator. He came to be actively involved—both in His day-to-day ministry and ultimately on the cross. He came to bear the consequences and pain of our brokenness and rebellion—and this leper becomes exhibit A of that brokenness.

How did Jesus respond? "Moved with compassion, Jesus stretched out His hand and touched him, and said to him, 'I am willing; be cleansed.' Immediately the leprosy left him and he was cleansed" (Mark 1:41–42).

"Moved with compassion" is a clear and appropriate expression of the heart of the Christ. His compassion is full-on compassion—not just pity that sees the sufferer and then recoils in shock. His is an active compassion that simply *must* engage the pain of this hurting man. And just as this man violated social taboos and prescriptive law by ignoring the crowd to get to Jesus, Christ places himself in what, to the watching crowd, would be the danger of ceremonial uncleanness.

He touches the leper! (See v. 41.)

This could easily seem like a throwaway detail, but it may actually be the most important element of the story. As we move through the inspired Gospels together in this book, we will find that Jesus had seemingly limitless ways of healing the hurting. He healed from nearby, and He healed from far away. He healed by word, and He healed by instructing the sufferer to do something remedial. Here, He heals with a touch—and that is what is so shocking!

Jesus could have healed the leper with a wave of the hand or a simple word. Or as Elisha did with Naaman of old, He could have ordered the leper to go bathe in the Jordan River (2 Kings 5). Instead, Jesus does something utterly unnecessary to the healing of the man's leprosy and absolutely necessary to the healing of the man's heart.

Remember, this man is in the final stages of leprosy. This means he has spent years in isolation. How long had it been since he shook a man's hand? If he had a family before being diagnosed with leprosy, how long had it been since he kissed his wife or hugged his children? Not only was leprosy a physical death sentence but it was also emotionally dehumanizing. Remember, the leper was "less-than." Not quite fully human anymore, he was a wraith who simply occupied space as he awaited death.

In Victor Hugo's classic book *The Hunchback of Notre Dame*, a badly deformed infant is taken to Paris where he is discovered by a priest who takes the child in. What is telling is the name the priest gives to the child—Quasimodo. According to *The Online Etymology Dictionary*, the name is made up of two Latin terms, whose possible meanings make for a tragic title. *Quasi* means "almost" and *modo* means "the measure of." Taken together, Quasimodo can mean "almost the measure of a human being"—almost a person. That captures well the experience of the leper, who has been trained to see himself as something less than human. And this is what makes Jesus's touch so compelling.

In a sense, it seems that the healing of the man's leprosy was, to Jesus, almost secondary to the healing of the man's heart. That simple touch, so unnecessary to the man's physical well-being, was absolutely essential to the man's emotional and spiritual welfare. With that warm, welcoming touch, the man was no longer alone. He was no longer isolated. He was no longer "almost a person." That divine touch was an invitation to rejoin the human race. The pain of rejection the man had known as an untouchable outcast was drawn away from his heart through the compassionate touch of the Christ.

In fact, Mark tells us that Jesus speaks to the man, saying, "I am willing; be cleansed" (1:41). Then the writer of this Gospel goes on to explain, "Immediately the leprosy left him and he was cleansed" (v. 42). The man was healed of his leprosy not by Jesus's touch, but by His words that followed the touch. The ceremonially unclean man was restored by Jesus, who, being sinless, is the very definition of ceremonial purity.

Clearly, Jesus's words provided relief from the leprosy, but His touch provided relief from the leper's loneliness. Jesus looked beyond the external and the obvious to the internal and the deep. He provided so much more than what the man greatly wanted, giving this leper what he truly needed—a restored place at the table of humanity.

A Lost Opportunity

Have you ever shared a story or a bit of information with someone—only to receive this response, "So, what's your point?" It can be frustrating and even a bit annoying. But it reminds us that we live in a bottom-line world where we are constantly looking for the Big Idea behind all of the so-called little ideas of life.

In the Scriptures, the Big Idea is Jesus and His mission of rescue, and all of the so-called "little ideas" in the stories of the Bible point to Him. In addition to pointing us to Jesus, this leper's encounter was intended to point to Him messianically in a larger, more missional sense.

This is clearly unveiled for us with the aftermath of the healing of the leper, for Mark adds an important postscript to the encounter:

> And He sternly warned him and immediately sent him away, and He said to him, "See that you say nothing to anyone; but go, show yourself to the priest and offer for your cleansing what Moses commanded, as a testimony to them." But he went out and began to proclaim it freely and to spread the news around, to such an extent that Jesus could no longer publicly enter a city, but stayed out in unpopulated areas; and they were coming to Him from everywhere. (Mark 1:43–45)

This is *not* routine. Jesus gives the man stern words of instruction, the strength of which are seen in the verbs:

- "Warned" (NASB) or "charged" (KJV), from a Greek word that means "to snort with anger"
- "Sent" can mean "excommunication" (though softer here, it is still intense)

These are strong words! But this is an opportunity the former leper fails to embrace. When Jesus sent him away, He told him to go to *the* priest and offer the sacrifice for a cleansed leper. Which priest? Perhaps it was the same one who had diagnosed this man's leprosy so many years before.

Why is this important? Because in the record of the Scriptures, until this moment there had not been a healed Jewish leper since the days of Miriam! Yes, Naaman the Syrian general had been healed in the days of Elisha, but Jesus himself would say of the uniqueness of that event, "And there were many lepers in Israel in the time of Elisha the prophet; and none of them was cleansed, but only Naaman the Syrian" (Luke 4:27). There were plenty of lepers, but healing had come to a foreigner. In the Old Testament record, only one leper was healed—Miriam.

Just as God had taken away the leprosy of Miriam, now Jesus has done what only God could do by removing leprosy from this man. It was time to offer the sacrifice for a cleansed leper—and it may have been the opportunity to offer that sacrifice for the first time in all of Jewish history.

What was that sacrifice? Notice Leviticus 14:2–7:

This shall be the law of the leper in the day of his cleansing. Now he shall be brought to the priest, and the priest shall go out to the outside of the camp. Thus the priest shall look, and if the infection of leprosy has been healed in the leper, then the priest shall give orders to take two live clean birds and cedar wood and a scarlet string and hyssop for the one who is to be cleansed. The priest shall also give orders to slay the one bird in an earthenware vessel over running water. As for the live bird, he shall take it together with the cedar wood and the scarlet string and the hyssop, and shall dip them and the live bird in the blood of the bird that was slain over the running water. He shall then sprinkle seven times the one who is to be cleansed from the leprosy and shall pronounce him clean, and shall let the live bird go free over the open field.

Few Old Testament sacrifices are described in such precise detail. This offering was pregnant with symbolism that would have had little meaning to Old Testament Israel. It was symbolism that anticipated the arrival of Jesus, the God-man. The bird slain in an earthen vessel can be seen as representing Jesus—who came in an earthen vessel (John 1:14, "became flesh") and was sacrificed in a human body for our sin and brokenness. This sacrifice happened over running water, picturing our sins being carried away forever. His blood, like that of the slain bird, is then applied to us, seen in the second bird. As a result, we are set free.

This sacrifice would become a portrait of the redeeming work of Christ as He sacrificed himself for us so we might be restored. The practice prescribed by the Old Testament could only be understood in the light of the Big Idea of the Bible—Jesus's sacrifice for a lost world.

Tragically, the leper disregards Jesus's command and goes around telling everyone of his rescue. And who can blame him? After years of isolation, he is now part of the community again. As a soul set free, he celebrates and bears witness to the work of Christ in His life. His actions are completely understandable, yet his failure to present himself to the priest as Jesus had instructed represented a lost opportunity to reveal the full identity of Jesus as God who came to walk among people on earth.

A Reversal of Positions

One Bible teacher noted a great irony here: The leper was told to tell no one, and he told everyone. We are told to tell everyone, but far too often we tell no one. But that is not the only case of role reversal we see here. For Jesus this event, in a sense, caused Him to trade places with the former leper. Luke's account says that after healing the man, Jesus went away to pray . . . alone (Luke 5:16).

The former leper is welcomed back into community while Jesus seeks the solitude of the wilderness. Amazing!

Still, even without the offering of the leper's sacrifice, the evidence has been clearly displayed. The Word had become flesh and had come to dwell among the people. What only God could do had been done by the Teacher from Nazareth. A day of wonder and rescue was upon the people—and it was captured in the heart of an untouchable who had been touched by the Heart that touches. Jesus's heart was well-described by the old gospel song:

> I heard the voice of Jesus say,
> "Come unto me and rest;
> Lay down, thou weary one, lay down
> Thy head upon my breast."
> I came to Jesus as I was,
> Weary, worn, and sad;
> I found in Him a resting place,
> And He has made me glad.
> —*Horatius Bonar, 1846*

A Heart That Marvels

Jesus and a Centurion

In one of the most famous conversations in human history, Roman governor Pontius Pilate stood before Jesus and asked the fascinating question, "What is truth?" (John 18:38). Then, as one writer put it, he did not stay to receive an answer. I have a different, even more fundamental question—what is faith?

A cursory cruise through the vast wilderness of the internet offers a wide variety of perspectives on the matter of faith. Philosopher Friedrich Nietzsche (1844–1900) wrote, "A casual stroll through the lunatic asylum shows that faith does not prove anything." And in case we didn't quite get what he was saying, he also said that faith is "not wanting to know what is true." Nineteenth-century preacher Henry Ward Beecher declared that "faith is nothing but spiritualized imagination." But faith must be pretty important contended pop singer George Michael (1963–2016), who crooned, "Yes, I've gotta have faith . . . faith . . . faith." If faith actually *is* important, Michelangelo (1475–1564) offered his own perspective on how it can matter, saying, "Faith in oneself is the best and safest course."

Of all the lines about faith I found in my slog through the web, however, the best statement came from theologian Thomas Aquinas (1225–1274), who wrote, "To one who has faith, no explanation is necessary. To one without faith, no explanation is possible." Oddly, the Bible seems to give its amen to such a slippery view by affirming, "Faith is the assurance of things hoped for, the conviction of things not seen" (Hebrews 11:1).

So where do we start in considering this idea of faith? Perhaps we can begin by considering the fact that the Bible underlines the significance of faith by telling us that we are saved *through faith* (Ephesians 2:8–9), we walk *by faith* (2 Corinthians 5:7), the just shall live *by faith* (Galatians 3:11), and that it is impossible to please God without *faith* (Hebrews 11:6).

With these verses in view, it might be valuable to take a closer look at this sometimes-fuzzy idea. To help in that endeavor, we will examine Jesus's encounter with a centurion—and we will watch as Jesus uses this soldier's confession to define true faith.

Setting the Stage

When I was in high school, I was in the drama club (responsible for helping with the lighting, not as one of the actors). Even though we had limited funds, equipment and, frankly, skill, we all understood that one of the keys to staging a good drama is getting the location and scene right. Every piece of furniture, every prop, and every costume were important parts of setting the stage so we could recreate the sense of place and usher those attending the play not only to their seat in the auditorium but also to the moment and location called for by the drama.

As we approach the story of Jesus and the centurion, the location is the Galilean fishing village of Capernaum. This story takes place directly after Jesus cleansed the leper, as we saw in chapter one. So Jesus descends the mount, and He is making His way toward Capernaum when He encounters the leper and interacts with the people we meet in this next story.

As we approach this event in the Gospels, we are given not only its location but also its timing. Remember that the New Testament gives us four distinctive gospel records, and each one has its own particular characteristics. As we have seen, Matthew, whose narrative includes both that leper and this centurion, seems to be the gospel writer who is most concerned about the chronology of the events he recorded.

Why is that significant here?

These two men—a leper and a soldier—come to Jesus right after He had presented the Sermon on the Mount. It bears repeating that the kingdom mandate Jesus had issued in that sermon is fresh in the minds of His listeners, perhaps causing them to wonder how to apply those teachings in challenging situations. Matthew then gives them two case studies: a marginalized Jewish leper and a gentile Roman soldier. In other words, to see how the kingdom operates, notice how it deals with those who have the least connection to it.

Additionally, we are privileged to have two different records of this encounter (Matthew 8:5–13 and Luke 7:1–10), with each supplying differing details that could be confusing unless they are wed together into one narrative. For instance, Matthew says that the centurion himself came to Jesus to make his request, but Luke says there were other players on stage in this drama. Let's start there:

> When He had completed all His discourse in the hearing of the people, He went to Capernaum. And a centurion's slave, who was highly regarded by him, was sick and about to die. When he heard about Jesus, he sent some Jewish elders asking Him to come and save the life of his slave. When they came to Jesus, they earnestly implored Him, saying, "He is worthy for You to grant this to him; for

he loves our nation and it was he who built us our synagogue." Now Jesus started on His way with them; and
when He was not far from the house, the centurion sent
friends, saying to Him, "Lord, do not trouble Yourself further, for I am not worthy for You to come under my roof;
for this reason I did not even consider myself worthy to
come to You, but just say the word, and my servant will be
healed." (Luke 7:1–7)

At the heart of the story is this centurion's concern for his
slave, who is extremely ill. Luke mentions that the elders of the
Capernaum synagogue approached Jesus to represent these con-
cerns to the Teacher and that these elders were followed by the
centurion's friends (perhaps other Romans?), who also requested
Jesus's intervention on behalf of the servant. Matthew's account
(8:5), however, says the centurion himself came to plead with Jesus
on the servant's behalf. How do we reconcile these clear differences?

Again, it is important to remember that the Gospels are not
biographies—they are inspired presentations demonstrating why
Jesus is the Son of God and why He deserves our trust. As such,
each gospel writer, targeting a distinctive audience, presents the
story of Jesus in a way that will help it to resonate with his audience. This means the writers may emphasize different details in the
same story because those details fit better with the way they are
trying to tell their audience about the Christ.

If you put the two accounts together, it is not difficult to imagine that both accounts are accurate although each is incomplete. It
is not unreasonable to read these encounters with Jesus as a series
of events, not two different events. The elders came to Jesus first.
They were followed by the centurion's friends, and in the end the
centurion himself shows up.

As we examine this series of encounters, several important things come to the surface. First, although this soldier is part of the Roman occupation force, he is not viewed and treated as one would normally expect. Throughout history, when a nation is conquered, the military force that defeated that country becomes an occupation force that is inevitably hated by the local people. The presence of the foreigners is a never-ending reminder that the local residents are a conquered people ruled by another country.

This centurion, though, is a different kind of occupier. He is respected and appreciated even by the Jewish religious leaders of Capernaum because in a very un-conquering-like way, he has gained a deep affection for the people of Capernaum—even building them a synagogue out of his own resources. This is the first of several indicators that reveal to us what a special individual this centurion was.

Second, the elders of the Capernaum synagogue seem to indicate that they think Jesus is capable of answering this man's request! They gladly approach Jesus and say that the centurion deserves to have his request granted by Jesus—a request they would not make if they didn't think it could happen.

Also, we should notice the mention of the Capernaum synagogue itself. Luke says that this was the synagogue the centurion had built and paid for, and it was the synagogue whose elders came to Jesus requesting this healing. But it also appears to be the same synagogue to which Jesus sent the cleansed leper in our previous encounter. When Jesus commanded the cleansed leper to go to the priest, the nearest synagogue—*this* synagogue—would have been the obvious choice.

Why does this matter? The lives of Matthew's Jewish audience focused on their religious observances of Judaism, and on a local level these observances were centered on the synagogue. It is there that they would have experienced the center of their community life, and it is there that they would have worshipped their God.

Matthew and Luke tie these events together with the thread of the synagogue to show the breadth of Jesus's kingdom values. Neither the most marginalized Jew nor the gentile soldier falls outside the kingdom mandates that Jesus had delivered—and now was living out.

Having seen the marginalized Jewish leper in the previous chapter, we need now to take a closer look at this Roman soldier.

A Soldier's Story

And when Jesus entered Capernaum, a centurion came to Him, imploring Him, and saying, "Lord, my servant is lying paralyzed at home, fearfully tormented." Jesus said to him, "I will come and heal him." (Matthew 8:5–7)

Marlene and I have a son in the military, and both of our dads served in World War II. I have been fascinated with the military all of my life, and talking with these men about their experiences has only heightened that interest.

War is one of the most consuming realities of our planet. One website claims that in the twentieth century alone, some one hundred sixty million people died because of a vast array of local or global conflicts. One of the great historic challenges of warfare, however, has been the thorny issue of winning the peace after you have won the war. When a war is finished, the conquered become the occupied and the conquerors become the occupiers. Soldiers do not necessarily make skilled police officers, which creates a significant tension between those two groups. That potential certainly existed between the occupying Roman garrison in the Galilean fishing village of Capernaum and its Jewish citizens.

Capernaum was not the only fishing village on the Sea of Galilee. Nor was it the most important community of the Galilee region. But it was the headquarters of Jesus's northern ministry—and it was a substantial enough community that a Roman garrison was billeted there. For a Roman officer, it would have been a backwater posting, far from the intrigue and political machinations of Jerusalem.

At the same time, Capernaum would have been a less stressful, more relaxed environment where the fears of battle could be set aside. This centurion had landed in Capernaum, and it would seem that the little fishing village had affected him in important ways. What can we know of him?

As a centurion, he would have been an officer in command of a century—one hundred troops. To compare them to today's army, centurions would have been similar to top sergeants. Centurions rose from the ranks based on merit. As a result, they generally constituted the best men in the Roman army. In fact, there are no less than seven centurions mentioned in the pages of the New Testament, and every one of them is spoken of with honor and respect. When you consider a centurion's role in leading a significant portion of Rome's occupation force, that is nothing short of stunning.

Beyond that, however, something seems to have captured the heart of this particular military man. Luke 7 says that the synagogue elders said of him, "He is worthy for You to grant this to him; for he loves our nation and it was he who built us our synagogue" (vv. 4–5). Centurions were blue-collar career types, and they tended not to be independently wealthy. Yet out of his own resources this centurion had funded the building of the Capernaum synagogue.

His motivation for that act? The declaration "he loves our nation" tells us everything we need to know about his heart. Far from the religious pomp and robed religious aristocracy of Jerusalem's temple, this man seems to have observed simple people with a simple faith in their invisible God, and he was struck by it. So struck, in fact, that he would find himself loving the people Rome had sent him to subdue.

But there is still more. Matthew 8:5–6 says, "And when Jesus entered Capernaum, a centurion came to Him, imploring Him, and saying, 'Lord, my servant is lying paralyzed at home, fearfully tormented.'" The "servant" is actually the Greek term *pais*, a tender, familial term for a boy, and Luke adds that this servant boy was "dear" to him. This concern sounds like a very normal thing to twenty-first century ears, but in the ancient Roman empire, it was far from a normal reaction.

Some scholars estimate that in Rome fifty percent of the total population consisted of slaves, and they were viewed as little more than property. If a slave got ill or died, the master pitched that person aside and got a new one. Slaves existed to be worked to death—with no feelings of remorse on the part of the masters. Ancient Roman writers confirm this:

- Gaius, a Roman legal expert: "It is unversally accepted that the master possesses the power of life and death over the slave."
- Varro: "The only difference between cattle, wagons, and slaves is that slaves can speak."
- Aristotle: "There can be no friendship or justice toward inanimate things; indeed not even toward a horse or an ox, nor yet towards a slave. A slave is a living tool, just as a tool is an inanimate slave."

Shockingly, however, this Roman cares. He cares enough to send emissaries with his request. But even more, this centurion cares so much that he himself—the conqueror—goes to this itinerant Rabbi—one of the conquered—to beg and plead on behalf of this servant. He, the powerful military occupier, humbles himself to intercede on behalf of the weak and the helpless.

Are there people in our daily experience who we too easily overlook—as if they weren't there or didn't matter? What about the person working the drive-through? The person you pay for fuel at the gas station? The custodian at church? The child next door?

Abigail Van Buren (Dear Abby) said, "The best index to a person's character is how he treats people who can't do him any good, and how he treats people who can't fight back." This brings us back to our friend the centurion. How did he treat "the least of these"? With a surprising depth of love and concern. I don't know what would have been more shocking to the watching crowd: the fact that this Roman officer went to Jesus on behalf of his servant or that Jesus received him.

Notice also what this officer says, "Lord, my servant is lying paralyzed at home, fearfully tormented," (Matthew 8:6). The fact that he called Jesus "Lord" may have shown a submission to Jesus's greater authority, or it may have simply been used as a sign of honor and respect.

What jumps off the page, however, is that in his statement no request is ever made. In today's military jargon, his words constitute a *sitrep*—a situation report. He does not presume to demand Jesus's intervention nor does he propose possible solutions. As a soldier reporting to his or her commander, this centurion simply states the situation and waits for Jesus to determine the best course of action.

A Statement of Faith

But the centurion said, "Lord, I am not worthy for You to come under my roof, but just say the word, and my servant will be healed. For I also am a man under authority, with soldiers under me; and I say to this one, 'Go!' and he goes, and to another, 'Come!' and he comes, and to my slave, 'Do this!' and he does it." (Matthew 8:8–9)

Sometimes we are tested when we don't get what we want. We lay our needs and requests before the God who loves us, and when we don't receive what we had hoped for our faith and confidence in God are tested. Why did God say no? Why did He say wait? Why did He remain silent? An apparent lack of response to our requests can deeply challenge our faith—especially when the situation is critical.

As I write this, a dear friend is sitting vigil with his cancer-ridden wife. Prayers from around the world have bombarded heaven on their behalf. Not only does she remain unhealed but she can't even gain the strength needed for chemotherapy or other vital treatments. The strongest faith would be challenged by God's apparent refusal to intervene in the life of a loved one.

Sometimes, however, we are tested when we get what we want. How will we react? How will this answer affect how we view our God or even how we view ourselves? When this centurion presents the need of his servant boy to Jesus, the Master's answer is as instantaneous as a lightning bolt, "I will come and heal him" (Matthew 8:7). How do you respond to that?

This Roman conqueror responds with a faith-filled humility that would have shocked everyone in the crowd. Hear his words again:

"Lord, I am not worthy for You to come under my roof, but just say the word, and my servant will be healed. For I also am a man under authority, with soldiers under me; and I say to this one, 'Go!' and he goes, and to another,

'Come!' and he comes, and to my slave, 'Do this!' and he does it." (Matthew 8:8–9)

He responds with a recognition of the authority of Jesus—and a concern that Jesus not be dishonored by whatever happens next. This centurion publicly affirms his confidence that Jesus's authority is absolute and that whatever the Master says will take place—no questions asked. He does it in a self-aware way. His self-assessment, "I am not worthy . . ." reveals a heart that understands its own frailty, especially as this man finds himself in the presence of the Christ.

But even more we see his concern. Jesus has agreed to go to the centurion's house where the sick boy lies. The centurion may have become a bit of a student of Judaism, because he seems to understand that if Jesus were to enter the home of a Gentile, He would be considered ceremonially unclean. The centurion's attitude? "I'm not worthy!" Again these are unexpected words for a Roman soldier to declare to a Jewish audience.

At the same time, however, he recognizes Jesus's authority. He affirms, "just say the word, and my servant will be healed" (Matthew 8:8). Considering that the New Testament frequently refers to Jesus as the *Logos*, the true Word of God (John 1:1, 14), it is as if the soldier is saying that *a* word from *the* Word is more than sufficient to meet this need. Location doesn't matter after all—it is all about the power and purposes of the Christ.

Put together, this soldier evidences a dependence on Christ that is breathtaking considering their respective positions in the community, and that remarkable display of trust is not lost on Jesus.

An Amazed Messiah
Now when Jesus heard this, He marveled and said to those

who were following, "Truly I say to you, I have not found such great faith with anyone in Israel." (Matthew 8:10)

What amazes you? Years ago, Paul McCartney wrote "Maybe I'm Amazed" as a love poem to his wife, Linda. Some years later, Academy Award–winning film director Steven Spielberg ventured into the realm of television long enough to tell a series of *Amazing Stories*. More close to our purposes, generations have reveled at former slave ship captain John Newton's hymn of praise "Amazing Grace." So, what amazes you?

Lots of things amaze me, but in this story, what amazes me is seeing Jesus amazed! After explaining the soldier's declaration of confidence in the ability and authority of Jesus, Matthew writes, "Now when Jesus heard *this,* He *marveled* and said to those who were following, 'Truly I say to you, I have not found such great faith with anyone in Israel'" (Matthew 8:10; emphasis added).

"He marveled." Fabulous words. *Marveled* is a Greek term that means, "to be in awe and wonder. To be amazed." Jesus was (and is) the Son of God, yet this soldier's statement of confident faith causes the Creator of the universe to be filled with amazement. But notice that it is not just the content of the centurion's words that causes Jesus to marvel but it is also the content of his heart. Listen to Jesus's public affirmation of this centurion to the watching Jewish crowd: "Truly I say to you, I have not found such great faith with anyone in Israel" (Matthew 8:10).

These words demand our attention. It seems clear that if Jesus had not found such faith in all of Israel, He must have been looking for it. He had looked among God's chosen people, the covenant nation of God. Israel: the people of the exodus and the Passover, the people of the Promised Land and the city of peace, the people of the law of Moses, and the people of the God of Abraham, Isaac,

and Jacob. The people had centuries of background and relationship with the God of heaven and earth—the Creator. Jesus had
come looking for faith, but He had found the wrong kind. He had
found faith in the law. Faith in the religious rituals. And faith in
the covenant without necessarily displaying faith in the God of
the covenant.

No, it was not a son or daughter of Abraham who had exhibited such "great faith." It was a Roman. A pagan. A Gentile. It was
an unnamed centurion who had learned to love the conquered
and care for a slave and publicly declare his confidence in Jesus of
Nazareth. It was a soldier whose heart was so completely trusting
in Jesus that Jesus saw what the crowd never could—and marveled at a faith so genuine that it showered the moment with love,
humility, trust, and compassion. It was a faith that had found its
object in the Rabbi who had just declared what a kingdom heart
looked like and then saw just such a heart standing before Him in
the most unlikely of circumstances.

◆ ◆ ◆

In the end Jesus granted the soldier's request and dispatched healing to the young servant boy (v. 13; from a distance, just as the
centurion had believed), and the soldier began to make his way
back home. However, as important as this miraculous healing was
to the servant and his master, it is not the key feature of the story.
Jesus had come looking for faith, and He found a gentile man of
war willing to profoundly place his trust in the Jewish Prince of
Peace. The fact of it is enough to challenge the imagination, but
the humility with which it was expressed was even more striking
than the faith itself.

In the story of the centurion and his servant boy, this must be seen. In Luke's account, the religious leaders said of the centurion, "He is worthy" (7:4) because they saw the deeds he had done. In Matthew's account the centurion has a very different self-view, declaring, "I am not worthy" (8:8) because he knew the true condition of his heart. But in words of affirmation and grace, Jesus responds to this man's need because He understands the true faith that is resident in this soldier's heart. True faith had infiltrated this centurion's life with the following:

- Transformed values of love and concern for others
- A humbled heart despite his position
- Submission to Christ's authority in his hour of need

I wonder. Do I make Jesus marvel? It is a challenging concept to wrestle with. But if your heart or mine is ever to amaze Him, it won't be because of our skill or talent or accomplishments or cleverness or wit or success or passion. It will be because we have learned to unequivocally place our trust in Him and His heart for us.

As the centurion returns to his home to be reunited with his dear servant boy, had this song been written, I am sure he would have enjoyed singing:

> 'Tis so sweet to trust in Jesus,
> Just to take Him at His Word;
> Just to rest upon His promise,
> Just to know, "Thus saith the Lord!"
> Jesus, Jesus, how I trust Him!
> How I've proved Him o'er and o'er;
> Jesus, Jesus, precious Jesus!
> O for grace to trust Him more!
> —*Louisa M. R. Stead, 1882*

THREE

A Heart That Accepts

Jesus and the Woman at the Well

In this day of creation care and environmental concern, we are continually encouraged to be good stewards of what we have. We are challenged to recycle, reuse, and so on. But still, we struggle with waste. Tons of trash, massive junkyards, and numerous companies based on recovering value from scrap all point to our cultural bent toward waste. According to *The Atlantic*, during one recent year the world was expected to generate 2.6 *trillion* pounds of garbage—the approximate weight of 7,000 Empire State Buildings. Clearly, we have become the "disposable generation."

In such a generation, it is easy for us to view people as being just as disposable as the rubbish we generate. Friendships, marriages, employees, children, and parents can all be seen as surplus when personal convenience and individual goals are at stake. If others hinder my opportunities for self-expression, self-advancement, or self-gratification, they become candidates for the trash heap.

By contrast, Jesus never wasted anything—a word, a moment, an effort, an opportunity. Or a person. In John 4, we find the Teacher stepping over numerous cultural boundaries and violating significant social taboos to give acceptance and value to a woman who has been thrown away over and over again. Not only will the Master not throw this woman away but He will also not waste the opportunity to have an impact on her heart for the kingdom. In fact, Jesus takes the initiative to open a door and show compassion to her hurting heart.

An Intentional Encounter

He left Judea and went away again into Galilee. And He had to pass through Samaria. So He came to a city of Samaria called Sychar, near the parcel of ground that Jacob gave to his son Joseph; and Jacob's well was there. So Jesus, being wearied from His journey, was sitting thus by the well. It was about the sixth hour. (John 4:3–6)

"He left Judea and went away again into Galilee" seems to be a simple, straightforward statement, but it is packed with cultural nuance. Standing between Judea to the south (complete with Jerusalem) and Galilee to the north (with Nazareth and Capernaum) was Samaria. Samaria was ancient Israel's equivalent to "No Man's Land" because "proper" Jews viewed its population as ethnically inferior.

The problems between Jews and Samaritans had a long history. In Old Testament times, following the death of King Solomon, the northern and southern regions of Israel split into two separate monarchies, ushering in the divided kingdom era for the people of God. The southern kingdom of Judah had Jerusalem as its capital, and the northern kingdom of Israel established its headquarters in the city of Samaria. The northern kingdom was eventually overrun by Assyria over a period of time ranging from 743 to 720 BC (see 2 Kings 15–18). Much of the population of the northern kingdom was carried away into exile, with a small resident population staying behind under the occupation force of the Assyrian conquerors. In the ensuing years, these populations intermarried, producing the ethnically mixed group that became known as Samaritans.

This ethnic impurity was the basis for Jewish disregard for their northern cousins. They considered the population of Samaria so unclean that when traveling from Judea to Galilee (or vice versa) observant Jews would avoid Samaria altogether. They would travel east across the Jordan River and travel north or south until they had passed the Samaritan territory. Then they would cross back over the Jordan and return to the homeland of ethnic Jews.

This is what makes John 4:4 so interesting, because John says, "And He *had* to pass through Samaria" (emphasis added). No, He actually didn't have to—and other Jews wouldn't. Yet not only does Jesus travel through this forbidden territory but He also does so with apparent purpose. There is a compulsion there that must be satisfied, and it would seem that what compels Jesus is His intent to meet this woman.

If that seems a bit of a stretch, consider this. John tells us that Jesus arrived at the famous well of Jacob on the outskirts of Sychar at the sixth hour. This would have been 12 noon—the most unlikely time to meet anyone at this well. But Jesus is there at the perfect time to salvage a throwaway life—for the now-famous Samaritan woman comes to draw water from Jacob's well at noon.

Again, this is remarkable because the normal custom was to draw water in the mornings and evenings when it was cooler. This woman is coming at the wrong time to the perfect place, and she encounters the Christ who *had* to pass through Samaria in order to meet her.

Why is she drawing water in the heat of the day? Why has she come alone? We will seek answers to those questions later in John 4—but make no mistake about it: This is not a chance encounter! Not a coincidence. Not serendipity. This is Jesus—perfectly orchestrating His movement to have a conversation with a woman whose life needs to be rescued from the trash heap.

An Open Door

Have you ever been in a situation where you committed a social or cultural *faux pas*? By the way, *faux pas* comes from French, and it means "false step." Dictionary.com defines it as "a slip or blunder in etiquette, manners, or conduct; an embarrassing social blunder or indiscretion"—and I have been guilty of that very thing more than once.

Years ago, as a young man, I was preaching in a small country church in the American West. The people were great and very informal, and I was trying to join in that casual spirit as I spoke. I went around the pulpit and placed my foot onto a railing at the front of the small platform. Instantly, everyone in the congregation became decidedly less casual. I could see them stiffen, and I could see on their faces that they were upset.

Why? Well, that rail where I put my foot was considered a "prayer altar." At the close of the services, the people would come there to pour out their hearts to God. In their minds, I dishonored prayer when I stuck my foot there. After the service, I was chastised repeatedly for what, truthfully, was an honest mistake. To them, though, I had committed a *faux pas* of the first order!

In John 4, Jesus has committed a social *faux pas* by traveling through Samaria instead of bypassing that region. Yet He goes even deeper into culturally unacceptable behavior by engaging not just a Samaritan in conversation but a Samaritan *woman*. Again, Jesus is doing this with intentionality in order to open the door for dialogue—in spite of the cultural taboos.

> And He had to pass through Samaria. So He came to a city of Samaria called Sychar, near the parcel of ground that Jacob gave to his son Joseph; and Jacob's well was there. So Jesus, being wearied from His journey, was sitting thus by

the well. It was about the sixth hour. There came a woman of Samaria to draw water. Jesus said to her, "Give Me a drink." For His disciples had gone away into the city to buy food. Therefore the Samaritan woman said to Him, "How is it that You, being a Jew, ask me for a drink since I am a Samaritan woman?" (For Jews have no dealings with Samaritans.) Jesus answered and said to her, "If you knew the gift of God, and who it is who says to you, 'Give Me a drink,' you would have asked Him, and He would have given you living water." (John 4:4–10)

Jesus develops common ground with this woman—the water of the well where they have met. When He requests a drink of water, her bitter, sarcastic response reveals the lonely sorrow of her heart. That response also displays the ethnic tension she has lived with for her entire life. Little does she know that a greater love than the one she has longed for—and failed to find—is standing before her.

Watch how Jesus exposes her deepest needs.

There appears to be more than a trace of sarcasm in the woman's reply in verses nine and ten, as if she meant, "To you Jews, Samaritans are trash. Why would you ask me for anything?" If so, it seems that Jesus paid no attention to her attitude. Why? He was more interested in winning the woman than He was in winning an argument.

As such, Jesus offers her something more than what she had come to draw from Jacob's well. He has come to offer the quenching of her spiritual thirstiness—a thirst she does not deny. Jesus is trying to pull her to higher ground, so she can look beyond the mundane, day-to-day need of the moment and see the more lasting and enduring need that remains unmet in her broken heart.

How does she respond?

The woman heard His words (vv. 11–12) but missed His meaning. To her, "living water" meant fresh spring water such as the well supplied. She could not understand how He could provide this water without having any means of drawing it from the well (even today the well is over seventy-five feet deep). Her comment was not surprising—she is locked into surface thinking and needs to be brought to a more holistic understanding of her actual needs and their eternal solutions.

Jesus's second reply (vv. 13–15) emphasized the contrast between the water in the well and what He intended to give. The material water would relieve thirst only temporarily, but the spiritual water He offered could quench her inner thirst forever. But she still isn't hearing Him. The well water was drawn up with hard labor, making her interests simple.

- All she *wanted* was something to save the effort of the long, hot trip from the village, but
- All she *needed* was the water of life—a subject John introduces here and then continues in John 7–8 (more on this in a later chapter).

As we have seen, Jesus doesn't waste anything. He will not throw away this woman, so He creates this moment to rescue her weary, broken heart. Notice how beautifully Jesus orchestrates this encounter to draw her heart out, just as she had come to pull water from the depths of the well. Jesus's personal work with her in this precise moment is part of the process of exposing the true needs that she doesn't want to come to grips with.

Strategic Timing. Although it was a woman's role to draw and carry the water, it was not normally done at noon. As we have seen, it was usually done in the early morning or late afternoon when it was cooler. This time at the well was also a social opportunity for the women of the village to set aside the burdens of the day for a few moments and spend time chatting with other women—a rare possibility in that era.

For this woman to be drawing water at noon may tell us much. It is possible that she had a sudden need for water, prompting this unusually timed visit to the well. As we will see, however, her past (vv. 16–18) offers a more likely option. It is probable that she had become an outcast and a social pariah in the community—especially among the women. As such, she would not care to meet the other women of the community, and they would have no interest in being with her. The other women no doubt shunned her—and as a result she finds herself alone with Jesus.

Spiritual Springboard. "Give Me a drink." Undoubtedly the woman was surprised to find a man sitting by the well. Jesus's initial approach was through a simple request for water—one would hardly refuse to give a drink of water to a thirsty traveler in the heat of the day. The request did have a surprising element, however, because no Jewish man (let alone a rabbi) would have condescended to drink from a Samaritan's cup (let alone volunteer to carry on a public conversation with a Samaritan woman). Some scholars think she may have actually wondered if the request was cover for a proposition—considering her past catalog of relational struggles.

Nevertheless, in His perfect wisdom Jesus identifies the Sahara of spirit this woman has been enduring. With the simple request for water for His thirst, He opens the way to offering her water for her thirsty soul—the mission on which He had come in the first place.

A Deep Loneliness

The abiding theme of popular music over the last fifty years is that of love. More songs speak of love than any other subject, whether it is the Beatles' classic "All You Need Is Love," Burt Bacharach and Hal David's hopeful "What the World Needs Now Is Love," or Roberta Flack's longing "Where Is the Love?" The desire for and pursuit of real love (and the fulfillment it can bring) have inspired some of the most poignant and touching lyrics ever penned.

The problem, however, is that this love is elusive. It is easier to pursue than it is to attain, and without it we find ourselves empty and alone. This becomes the seedbed for yet more music, and this music cuts to the deepest pain of the heart—the pain of longing for a true, meaningful relationship and finding those hopes and dreams dashed. Songs like "Mr. Lonely," "I'm So Lonesome I Could Cry," "Hey There Lonely Girl," and the haunting "A House Is Not a Home" all speak to the heartache of doing life alone.

The emptiness of finding yourself utterly alone is a pain we understand—and fear deeply. The woman Jesus is encountering is arguably a truly lonely person—pictured by her trail of broken relationships and her coming to the well at noon.

Now Jesus will begin breaking through her loneliness and begin drawing her into the most important and enduring relationship any person could ever know—a relationship with the Creator.

> She said to Him, "Sir, You have nothing to draw with and the well is deep; where then do You get that living water? You are not greater than our father Jacob, are You, who gave us the well, and drank of it himself and his sons and his cattle?" Jesus answered and said to her, "Everyone who drinks of this water will thirst again; but whoever drinks of the water that I will give him shall never thirst; but the

water that I will give him will become in him a well of water springing up to eternal life."

The woman said to Him, "Sir, give me this water, so I will not be thirsty nor come all the way here to draw." He said to her, "Go, call your husband and come here." The woman answered and said, "I have no husband." Jesus said to her, "You have correctly said, 'I have no husband'; for you have had five husbands, and the one whom you now have is not your husband; this you have said truly." (John 4:11–18)

Now Jesus digs deeper into this woman's life. He must get to the heart of the matter—which is the emptiness of her heart. As He does so, He displays more than just insightful teaching. Jesus displays His deep understanding by revealing her inner turmoil and confusion.

Moral Confusion (vv. 16–18). Jesus's request to call her husband was both proper and strategic. It was proper because in that day it was not good etiquette for a woman to talk with a man unless her husband was present. It is only fitting that a man of good motives and proper intent would protect the woman's reputation (and his own) by keeping her husband within the realm of the conversation.

However, Jesus's question about her husband was also strategic because it placed her in a dilemma from which she could not free herself without admitting her need. She had no husband she could call, and she would not want to confess her relational failures to a stranger. The abruptness of her reply ("I have no husband") shows that she was emotionally conflicted. It had to have been shocking to the woman when Jesus lifted the curtain on her past life.

With Jesus's question and the woman's response, the conversation now passes from small talk to an intensely personal discussion. We don't know the nature of her many marriages, nor do we know why they kept ending prematurely. What we do know is that she kept trying, kept searching, and kept longing for a relationship of substance to fill the emptiness of her heart. Jesus drills down into this longing by affirming that, yes, she currently has no husband. After having gone through five marriages, she is now living with a man outside the framework of marriage.

If, as some scholars have suggested, she had been running away by moving from one relationship to another, she has not found what she was longing for. If she was continually being thrown away, the result was the same. She has only continued to find herself alone. Jesus moves into this relational vacuum and exposes her to a new kind of relationship—with God through Him.

A Welcome into Relationship

What do politics and religion have in common? For one thing, in social gatherings they are generally off-limits for discussion because they are such polarizing issues. These are subjects that create moments of awkward silence, moments of rising anger, or moments of indignation that can spoil the atmosphere of a party. Why?

These subjects far too often generate more heat than light and are usually pointed toward winning the debate rather than gaining understanding. Having said that, conversations about religion can also become an effective dodge when the pointed end of a conversation hits too close to home and becomes uncomfortable—which is what may be in view in Jesus's conversation with the woman at Jacob's ancient well. Jesus's clear understanding of her life-situation prompts a change of subject for the woman at the well in Sychar. To move away from the intensely personal, she tries to turn the conversation to more neutral ground—religion.

> The woman said to Him, "Sir, I perceive that You are a prophet. Our fathers worshiped in this mountain, and you people say that in Jerusalem is the place where men ought to worship." Jesus said to her, "Woman, believe Me, an hour is coming when neither in this mountain nor in Jerusalem will you worship the Father. You worship what you do not know; we worship what we know, for salvation is from the Jews. But an hour is coming, and now is, when the true worshipers will worship the Father in spirit and truth; for such people the Father seeks to be His worshipers. God is spirit, and those who worship Him must worship in spirit and truth." The woman said to Him, "I know that Messiah is coming (He who is called Christ); when that One comes, He will declare all things to us." Jesus said to her, "I who speak to you am He." (John 4:19–26)

She responds to Jesus's uncomfortably personal probing by dodging the issue. Rather than allowing this awkward conversation to go deeper into her relational failures, she tries to make Jesus the issue—and calls Him a prophet (v. 19).

If in fact this was an attempt to dodge the discussion of her past marriages, she unwittingly has moved their chat into the direction of her real need—her deepest heart need: her need of a relationship with God. That relationship will replace her religious emptiness, which is just as profound as her relational loneliness.

The woman at the well tries to move the dialogue away from her past by debating the old controversy between Jews and Samaritans, and whether proper worship should be offered on Mount Gerizim, in Samaria, or at Jerusalem, where the Jewish temples had been built. If it was a ploy, it would fail. Jesus is after her heart—not her religious pedigree. To get there, she needs to know Him and discover that He is exactly what she needs. She must learn that He is sufficient.

Sufficient for Clarity (v. 22). Jesus avoided the argument by elevating the issue above mere location. He made no concessions, and He intimated that the Samaritans' worship was confused: "You [Samaritans] worship what you do not know." He was referring perhaps to earlier generations of Samaritans, who had practiced syncretism by mixing the worship of foreign idols with that of Jehovah. True worship is that of the Spirit, which means that the worshiper must deal honestly and openly with the one true God.

Sufficient for Relationship (vv. 23–24). "God is spirit, and his worshipers must worship in the Spirit and in truth" (NIV). Jesus was explaining to her that God cannot be confined to one place nor be conceived of in finite, material ways—but that He is nevertheless knowable. Only "the Word [that] became flesh" (see John 1:14) could represent Him and give us access to Him, and that is why Jesus came. He came to make the Father known and to give us access to that Father.

This aspect of Jesus's mission was used as a preface to John's entire gospel record. Although Jesus would be rejected by His own, the offer of a new relationship with the Father was available to all—including this Samaritan woman.

He was in the world, and the world was made through Him, and the world did not know Him. He came to His own, and those who were His own did not receive Him.

But as many as received Him, to them He gave the right to become children of God, even to those who believe in His name, who were born, not of blood nor of the will of the flesh nor of the will of man, but of God. (John 1:10–13)

This mission statement was being lived out at a well near Sychar as Jesus offered this woman the opportunity for a relationship with God that her ethnically proud cousins in Israel were largely rejecting.

Sufficient for Understanding (vv. 25–26). Mystified by Jesus's words, the woman finally confessed her ignorance and at the same time expressed her longing, "I know that Messiah . . . is coming. When he comes, he will explain everything to us" (v. 25 NIV). It was the one faint hope she had of finding God, finding meaning, finding love. She expected the coming Messiah to explain the mysteries of life.

On this sincere (though vague) hope, Jesus based His appeal to her heart. This is the one occasion when Jesus openly, clearly, and voluntarily declared His messiahship. The Synoptic Gospels show that, as a general rule, He did not make such a public claim of His true identity. In fact, Jesus often urged His disciples to say nothing about who He truly was (Matthew 16:20; Mark 8:29–30; Luke 9:20–21). Yet to this woman He openly declares His true identity, saying in essence: "You are looking for Messiah? Here I am!"

Why? Because this lonely Samaritan was part of the mission He had received from His Father.

Living with Purpose

What do you live for? What gets you up in the morning and keeps you going all day long? What is it that really winds your watch?

For some it is their career. For others, their family. For still others, it is sports or hobbies or causes or any number of things that, at their very best, give us a sense of purpose and fulfillment in life. What's yours?

For Jesus, however, His purpose and fulfillment came from one pristine idea—pleasing the Father. After Jesus took the woman at the well to the very doorstep of renewed relationship with the one true God, the conversation is now abruptly interrupted. His disciples return from the village.

> At this point His disciples came, and they were amazed that He had been speaking with a woman, yet no one said, "What do You seek?" or, "Why do You speak with her?" So the woman left her waterpot, and went into the city and said to the men, "Come, see a man who told me all the things that I have done; this is not the Christ, is it?" They went out of the city, and were coming to Him.
>
> Meanwhile the disciples were urging Him, saying, "Rabbi, eat." But He said to them, "I have food to eat that you do not know about." So the disciples were saying to one another, "No one brought Him anything to eat, did he?" Jesus said to them, "My food is to do the will of Him who sent Me and to accomplish His work. Do you not say, 'There are yet four months, and then comes the harvest'? Behold, I say to you, lift up your eyes and look on the fields, that they are white for harvest. (John 4:27–35)

It seems pretty clear that the disciples are shocked to see their teacher in conversation with a woman—let alone one who is ethnically impure. But as they arrive, she leaves with a completely different perspective from the one she had brought with her to the well.

Notice the impact of her encounter with Jesus:

- She leaves her waterpot behind and goes back to Sychar (v. 28). When she had come, the waterpot was central to her mission and the reason she had come to the well. Now it is incidental. She is on a different mission.
- She declares Christ to the men of the town (v. 29). Some argue that her past may have gotten their attention. If Jesus had exposed "all the things that she had done" what might that expose about them? But whatever was in their hearts, they not only listen to the woman's claims but they also respond to them and . . .
- Many come to Christ, longing for Him to stay among them (vv. 39–42). Unlike many others in Israel, who rejected Jesus when He came to the Samaritan village of Sychar, they received Him, and upon hearing His words, they believed in Him. The Samaritans gladly embraced what the Jews have failed to understand—the Savior had come.

◆ ◆ ◆

Jesus declares that in this He has accomplished His purpose in coming into the world—to do His Father's will (v. 34) and to reap a harvest of men and women (v. 35), including the woman He had met at Jacob's well. But think about this encounter with this hurting woman.

- Think how easily He could have ignored her—her pain was her problem.
- Think how easily He could have ignored her—she was racially inferior.

- Think how easily He could have ignored her—she was not one of the beautiful people. Her life was a spiritual and moral mess.
- Think how easily He could have ignored her—she responded to Him with bitterness and sarcasm, not faith and appreciation.

But He did *not* ignore her. He saw the pain and loneliness of her heart, and He probed it—not to hurt her but to bring her to the love and relationship she so desperately wanted but had failed to find. Jesus's compassion—piercing and reaching and touching—evidences His great heart of acceptance of the outcast and alone, the less-than, and the unloved.

And that was the point. In a world that excludes and separates and divides and ignores, Jesus accepts. Because that is why He came.

> But when Jesus heard this, He said, "It is not those who are healthy who need a physician, but those who are sick. But go and learn what this means: 'I DESIRE COMPASSION, AND NOT SACRIFICE,' for I did not come to call the righteous, but sinners." (Matthew 9:12–13)

The question we must face is this: Are we ready, like Jesus, to reach out to the person whose life is a wreck, who doesn't have it all together, whose heart is an empty shell, and whose needs are high maintenance? As Jesus reaches out to this woman of loneliness, He raises the bar on compassion. Will we join Him in that compassion for the lonely and forgotten, or will we ignore those He longs to accept?

Charles Wesley's words speak profoundly of this love, not only for us but also for those on the fringes of life to whom Jesus offers relationship and love and care:

Other refuge have I none;
Hangs my helpless soul on Thee;
Leave, ah! Leave me not alone,
Still support and comfort me.
All my trust on Thee is stayed,
All my help from Thee I bring;
Cover my defenseless head
With the shadow of Thy wing.
                    —*Charles Wesley, 1740*

FOUR

A Heart That Cares
Jesus and Two Daughters

Waiting has to be one of life's most familiar, yet difficult, experiences. We wait in doctor's offices, at traffic lights, in the drive-through line, for payday's arrival, for a loan approval, even for answers to our prayers. Nothing makes us feel so helpless as waiting. As a result, few things are so utterly challenging to us.

My dad was forty when he had his first major heart attack, a byproduct of becoming a smoker during his World War II Navy years and of eating foods laden with too much fat. It was a massive cardiac event, after which the doctor told us he didn't know another man who would have survived it—let alone being able to walk several blocks to the parking lot to retrieve his car and then drive himself twenty minutes to the hospital and ask someone to contact his physician.

From the moment he had that heart attack, it seemed as if Dad was on the clock. He was waiting, and we were waiting with him. Mom lived with the constant fear that his next attack—and he would have several—would be the one that would take him. We kids wondered what we needed to do to take up the slack and relieve him of pressure in an attempt to forestall that killer blow.

Over the course of the next eighteen years or so, we waited. We watched as he experienced deteriorating health, permanent work disability, loss of strength, and a personality hardened by cardiovascular issues that created multiple TIA strokes (mini-strokes), sometimes on a daily basis.

And we waited. Waited for a medical miracle. Waited for another episode. Waited, as if the sword of Damocles were dangling above our collective heads with the string fraying before our eyes. Waiting for what seemed inevitable. And we waited knowing there was nothing we could do to prevent that inevitability. The dreadful waiting ended on June 3, 1980, when the final, fatal cardiac arrest took my dad. He was only fifty-eight years old, and almost a third of his life had been spent waiting for the other proverbial shoe to drop.

When we are "in the waiting," as Shannon Wexelberg sings in her album *Story of My Life*, our emotions swing between hope and terror, possibility and despair, faith and doubt. We live under the pressure of not knowing if relief will ever come or if our worst fears will be realized.

Such would have been the emotional ups and downs of two people Jesus encountered in Mark 5—one whose wait seems to have been relatively brief, and the other who had carried her cares for a dozen long years. One battled for the daughter he deeply loved and the other was in the waiting for her own health needs. At risk and in the waiting were these two daughters.

A Matter of Value

A term familiar to today's world is "planned obsolescence." No longer are things designed and manufactured to last, but they are designed to be replaced. Think for a minute about all the things that are made to be thrown away—disposable razors, water bottles, lighters, and more.

This disposable culture is also reflected in more significant ways—with relationships seeming to be commitment-optional in many areas of our society. Marriages struggle to survive; long-term employees are discharged ahead of retirement for lower-priced options; and highly regarded athletes change teams seemingly as often as they change their socks, with the result that we end up cheering for the name on the front of the jersey and not the one on the back.

Interestingly, this characteristic of the modern world was also a significant part of the culture of ancient Rome. It has been called an "abandonment" culture, and that culture had a profound effect on women. It is widely known that in the Roman world women were seen to have little or no value. A song James Brown would make popular in the 1960s: "It's a Man's World," could have been the anthem of the Roman Empire. And some understanding of that empire and its view of women can provide context for this event.

Of first consideration is the fact that, as we have seen, each of the four Gospels was written to present Christ in a specific way to a specific target audience. For instance, Matthew wrote to a Jewish audience to affirm Jesus as the King of the Jews, quoting the Old Testament liberally. Meanwhile, Luke's audience was Greek, and education and philosophy were key ingredients in the Greek culture. Little wonder then that Luke gives us so many of Jesus's parables and so much of His core teaching.

Why does this matter? Scholars largely agree that Mark's gospel account was written to a primarily Roman audience. His record is an action-packed telling of the story of Jesus with almost non-stop demonstrations of the miraculous—healings from diseases, deliverance from demons, resurrection from death. This Roman audience would have heard Mark's account against the backdrop of their culture, and that culture had some nasty characteristics.

One common Roman practice codified into Roman law was

called "exposure." When a family was expecting the birth of a child, the father had absolute authority over the life of that child. When the baby was born, the child would be brought and laid at the feet of his or her father. If the father picked up the child and held it, that infant would be welcomed as part of the family. If, however, the father turned away from the child, that baby would be taken to the woods or the city garbage heap and abandoned—exposed to the elements or the wild animals—and left to die. Sociologist and historian Rodney Stark points out that one of the things that distinguished the first-century church from its surrounding culture was the fact that followers of Christ would routinely rescue these abandoned babies—male or female—and raise them to live full lives.

Part of the concept of exposure, however, was that the father could reject the child for any number of reasons, including birth defects. One of the primary motivations for abandoning a child to exposure was if that baby was a little girl. The Roman culture had a very utilitarian view of women (as did much of the ancient world, including Israel) and saw their value, primarily, as producing more male babies. In a culture of exposure and abandonment, female babies were optional.

This is how lowly the women of the Roman-dominated first century were viewed, yet as Mark writes to a Roman audience he tells a story that features Jesus's care for two females. All by itself, this would have been a shock to the first hearers of Mark's gospel. Those for whom the culture had little or no use were of value to the Rabbi from Nazareth. This constituted a shocking exposure of a different kind, for it exposed the reality that Jesus had a heart for people seen as having little or no value.

As we consider this pair of encounters with Jesus, we'll see that these two females are linked together. It is no accident that their stories are told together, for they are connected both by the action of the story and by the actions of the Christ. We will see the events as if Mark is giving us a drama in three acts. Act One, which may have been a surprise to the Roman first hearers of Mark's gospel, focuses on a father who is desperate to save his little daughter.

Act One: A Desperate Dad

When Jesus had crossed over again in the boat to the other side, a large crowd gathered around Him; and so He stayed by the seashore. One of the synagogue officials named Jairus came up, and on seeing Him, fell at His feet and implored Him earnestly, saying, "My little daughter is at the point of death; please come and lay Your hands on her, so that she will get well and live." And He went off with him; and a large crowd was following Him and pressing in on Him. (Mark 5:21–24)

There are two kinds of suffering in this world—and both can be overwhelming. There is primary suffering, when the individual is the sufferer and feels the anguish of the pain. There is also secondary suffering—when the sufferer is someone you love. As a parent, I don't know that there is anything worse than watching your child suffer while realizing there is nothing you can do to relieve that suffering. That is the situation Jairus faces as he comes to Jesus to plead for his suffering daughter.

Jesus had been across the Galilee to the eastern shore in the region of the Decapolis (ten cities built by the Roman Empire) where he had just rescued a demon-possessed man from a "legion" of evil spirits. The result of that divine act of rescue? The people of the region begged Jesus to leave their territory! (v. 17). I wonder if the terror they experienced in the presence of the demon-possessed man did not compare to the terror of encountering Someone with the power to command those demons. So Jesus and His men cross back to the west shore of the Galilee (v. 21), and a large crowd—as was increasingly becoming the case—was waiting for Him to arrive back in Capernaum (v. 21).

Part of that welcoming committee was a man named Jairus. The fact that Jairus was an official of the Capernaum synagogue (built by the centurion we met in chapter 2) is significant. By the time we have moved into Mark 5, the popularity of Jesus is growing widely, but He is also beginning to be watched with concern by the religious leaders.

Jairus was one of those leaders, perhaps even one of the elders of the synagogue who had intervened on behalf of the centurion. Now he comes to Jesus and humbles himself before the Rabbi. Notice how Mark describes the actions of this man:

- **"fell at His feet"** This is a position of humility, and often it is one presented as a position of worship. While it may be unlikely that worship was in his heart, it is clear that Jairus is not the least bit hesitant to publicly humble himself before Jesus. Such is the depth of his love and concern for his daughter. While Jairus's concern for his female child may have been surprising to some Romans, for this community leader to so abase himself before a traveling rabbi would certainly have shocked the Jewish crowd gathered at the shore of Galilee that day. For Jairus, though, his pride and his position in the community are nothing when compared to his little girl's desperate need.

- **"implored Him earnestly"** Hear the words he uses: "My little daughter." This bespeaks a heart of love mingled with pain. It is such a tender, sweet phrase and it expresses a depth of care for a daughter that, while not unique or novel in that day, certainly stood in striking contrast to the Roman culture of abandonment.

Jairus's daughter is dying—and he is convinced that Jesus is her only hope. This mission of mercy was rewarded by Jesus's willingness to go home with this hurting father and rescue the joy of his heart.

Act Two: A Desperate Woman

And He went off with him; and a large crowd was following Him and pressing in on Him. A woman who had had a hemorrhage for twelve years, and had endured much at the hands of many physicians, and had spent all that she had and was not helped at all, but rather had grown worse—after hearing about Jesus, she came up in the crowd behind Him and touched His cloak. For she thought, "If I just touch His garments, I will get well." Immediately the flow of her blood was dried up; and she felt in her body that she was healed of her affliction. Immediately Jesus, perceiving in Himself that the power proceeding from Him had gone forth, turned around in the crowd and said, "Who touched My garments?" And His disciples said to Him, "You see the crowd pressing in on You, and You say, 'Who touched Me?'" And He looked around to see the woman who had done this. But the woman fearing and trembling, aware of what had happened to her, came and fell down before Him and told Him the whole truth. And He said to her, "Daughter, your faith has made you well; go in peace and be healed of your affliction." (Mark 5:24–34)

My favorite poem, attributed to the ancient Greek poet Aeschylus, speaks about the human condition and suffering—and challenges us to acknowledge that in suffering we are forced to look to our God, His wisdom, and His ways. Aeschylus wrote:

> Even in our sleep, pain which cannot forget,
>   Falls drop by drop upon the heart,
>   Until, in our own despair, against our will, comes wisdom
>   Through the awful grace of God.

That is the case with this diseased woman. She is driven to Jesus as the only possible source of relief for her suffering; consequently, Jairus was not the only desperate person in that crowd. In fact, you could make a convincing case that almost everyone there was exhibiting some measure of desperation. In verse 24, Mark describes the scene as almost frantic. He says that the crowd was "pressing in on Him," but those words don't do justice to the scene. Some translations say that they "thronged" Him, but that sounds a bit dated to our ears. The word that best captures the press of this mob for our understanding is that they were *suffocating* Him. Because the crowd was pressing Him in from all sides, it is likely that Jesus and Jairus could barely breathe, let alone move.

Nevertheless, of all the desperate people in that mob, only one person's panic rose to the same level as that of Jairus. While Jairus was desperate because of the pain of someone else, the woman who approached Jesus through the crowd was struggling with her own pain. Who was she? Historically, she has been known as the "woman with the issue of blood." Beyond that, the Gospels give us nothing by which to identify her, and her anonymity within the narrative is almost a reflection of the culture's view of women.

Her problem? A bloody hemorrhage she had suffered ("endured") for twelve years. Two factors about this condition are brutal, and they are vital to our understanding of her experience. First, there was no medical solution to her condition. And, believe me, she had tried. Mark tells us that she had spent these twelve years consulting physicians, who not only could not heal her but they also made her condition increasingly debilitating! Their treatments bordered on the superstitious and offered no relief whatsoever.

To make it worse, even though the doctors could not stop her physical bleeding, they bled her dry of all her resources. They bankrupted her without providing any help. You can't miss Mark's cynicism with first-century medical practices as he describes her situation. By contrast, physician Luke simply said she was incurable—with no reference to the victimization Mark describes. That view would have sung harmony with the general consensus of the day. Ancient rabbinical teaching declared, "The best physician is worthy only of Gehenna." I doubt this woman would have disagreed.

Second, this was likely a menstrual hemorrhage in which she bled constantly. The two results of this discharge would have been shattering to a woman of that day. First, she would be in a constant state of ceremonial uncleanness (Leviticus 15:19–25). And second, she would have been rendered useless for the one thing women were valued for—childbearing. As a result, according to rabbinical teaching, a woman with an ongoing menstrual hemorrhage would be a social pariah whose life would be eerily similar to the leper we saw in chapter one. The rabbinic teaching said that she could be:

- Excommunicated from both temple and synagogue activities,
- Divorced from her husband,

- Shut out of family life,
- Ostracized from community life.

For a dozen years, this has been her experience. It's not enough that she has suffered from this disease and its ever-weakening impact, but she had also been emotionally and spiritually abused by the very community she should have been able to turn to for help. So with no place left to go, she turns to Jesus. Her thinking? "If I just touch His garments, I will get well" (Mark 5:28). The Greek word that is translated "get well" is *sozo*, meaning "made whole."

To the twenty-first-century ear, this sounds almost superstitious, but for her it was a last hope. A lifeline. One final attempt to be normal again. And the degree of her desperation is evidenced by the struggle she would have endured just to fight her way through the crowd to get to Jesus at all. In her weakened condition, forcing her way through this suffocating mob would have been extraordinarily difficult, yet she claws her way forward, continuing to recite her internal mantra, "If I just touch His garments . . ."

What a contrast to the leper we saw in chapter one. There Jesus touched the leper, but here the desperate woman touches Jesus—and the instant that touch occurs, her hemorrhage dries up. Power flows from Jesus to her (vv. 29–30) and she is healed. The Greek tense used is absolute. It speaks of a complete, immediate, and permanent cure, and she instantly knew it. She could tell. Her perpetual weakness had been replaced by renewed strength. Where she had been debilitated and drained, now she was well.

As you read the story, you get the feeling that once she was healed, this woman sought to silently fade away into the background. Jesus, however, wants the world to know that she is restored. He stops the crowd in mid-journey and asks what, to His disciples, seemed like an odd question. He asked, "Who touched Me?" With the push and pull of the mob, He was being touched on every side! Yet, this purposeful touch needed attention.

Though some Bible teachers disagree, I don't think Jesus asked the question because He didn't know the answer. Power had gone from Him, and that power had accomplished something miraculous. Her healing would allow a subsequent reinstatement to the community. This should be made public. I would suggest that He asked the question because He wanted her to declare her healing and begin the process of social restoration.

The woman, however, was terrified because she had violated social taboos to come to Jesus in this crowd. Because of her condition, she had been expelled from community life. By the letter of the law, every person she had touched in her battle to get to Jesus would have instantly become ceremonially unclean. Her audacious act, while securing her healing, would have been seen as a violation against the community. Mark was right to say that she was "fearing and trembling" (v. 33). She has been exposed. But when summoned by her Rescuer, she steps forward and owns what she has done, falling at Jesus's feet—exactly the same posture Jairus had struck in verse 22.

Her fears were unnecessary. Jesus looks at her and calms her heart by calling her "daughter." Keep in mind that the last time this crowd heard that word, it fell from the lips of Jairus, imbued with all his love, concern, and passion for his suffering little girl. By using that word in this context, Jesus is putting in front of the crowd the same heart for this hurting woman that Jairus had displayed for his little girl!

We can add to the significance of this moment by noting that although Jesus encountered countless women throughout the gospel records, this is the only time He calls a woman "daughter."

Warmth. Affection. Acceptance. Care. Love. The offer of peace (v. 34). All wrapped up in the simple word, "Daughter."

Church tradition offers a fascinating theory on this woman's identity. Although this cannot be proven, tradition says that her name was Veronica and that after her healing she became a follower of Jesus. In fact, the tradition says that she followed the Master all the way to His cross.

The Via Dolorosa (the Way of Suffering) in Jerusalem is the traditional name of Jesus's journey to the cross from Pilate's court, and it is marked liturgically by the "stations of the cross"—road markers along the way where things happened either in the Scriptures or in tradition. Station 6 points us to this Veronica, who offers Jesus her veil to wipe the blood from His face. If this tradition is true, it is a beautiful act of mercy to dry the blood of the Healer who months before had stanched her own bloody discharge.

Now the rescued woman goes her way whole, and Jairus once again wants Jesus to come to his home to rescue his daughter.

Act Three: A Dramatic Rescue

While He was still speaking, they came from the house of the synagogue official, saying, "Your daughter has died; why trouble the Teacher anymore?" But Jesus, overhearing what was being spoken, said to the synagogue official, "Do not be afraid any longer, only believe." And He allowed no one to accompany Him, except Peter and James and John the brother of James. They came to the house of the synagogue official; and He saw a commotion, and people loudly weeping and wailing. And entering in, He said to them, "Why make a commotion and weep? The child has not died, but is asleep." They began laughing at Him. But putting them all out, He took along the child's father

and mother and His own companions, and entered the
room where the child was. Taking the child by the hand,
He said to her, "Talitha kum!" (which translated means,
"Little girl, I say to you, get up!"). Immediately the girl
got up and began to walk, for she was twelve years old.
And immediately they were completely astounded. And
He gave them strict orders that no one should know about
this, and He said that something should be given her to
eat. (Mark 5:35–43)

For twelve years, the suffering woman had been in the waiting—longing for relief and rescue. But the instant Jesus stops the
procession and turns to interact with her, Jairus is suddenly placed
in the waiting.

It doesn't take a massive amount of biblical imagination to enter
into the mind of Jairus as all this has been going on. A dad as
concerned as he clearly is must have gone a bit crazy at the delay
caused by the woman's act. If it were me, my voice might be silent,
but my mind would be screaming, "What are you doing? We don't
have a second to spare. We have to keep moving, or else my daughter is lost!"

Such a response would be perfectly normal, and if that is what
Jairus was thinking, his worst nightmares were about to be realized. As Jesus concludes His conversation with the woman, a mes-
senger comes from Jairus's home with the heart-shattering news
that the child is gone. It's too late. There's no point in continuing
any farther.

Jairus's momentary sense of hope that arose when Jesus agreed
to come has now evaporated. Now there was only grief and loss.
The immeasurably painful empty ache of a parent comes when
that parent has to bury a child. Our children are supposed to

bury us—it's not right and it's unnatural when it's the other way around.

Jesus, however, is undaunted by the news. He assures Jairus that all will be well, and they continue on to the home where the ceremonial mourners had already set up camp and had begun to wail with grief over the loss. When Jesus informs them that the child is not dead, their cries of grief turn to sardonic laughter. The cries of their lips and the sarcasm in their hearts may have even found a foothold in Jairus's heart as well.

Jesus, accompanied by His inner circle of disciples (Peter, James, John) plus Jairus and his wife, enters the room where the girl lay. Just as Jesus had gently dealt with the woman earlier, His call to the little girl is rich with tenderness, saying, "Talitha kum." Mark translates the Aramaic for us, "Little girl, get up!" It wasn't the time for sleeping, and it wasn't a day for dying. In the presence of the One who is the resurrection and the life, it was a day for restoration. Just as the woman had been restored, the little girl rises and is restored to her parents.

I love the practicality of Jesus. Instead of calling for a praise rally to celebrate the event or a press conference to publicize the miracle, Jesus simply tells them to give her something to eat. Apparently, being dead works up a bit of an appetite! The astonishment of the parents and the crowd was spectacular, but our own astonishment shouldn't be far behind.

Mark's closing footnote says simply that the little girl was twelve years old—the exact amount of time the woman with the hemorrhage had been ill. These two daughters are linked together by the miraculous Christ and by their own experiences, but in reverse. As the woman had known twelve years of isolation, pain, and struggle, Jairus had known twelve years of joy with his little girl. And just as the woman's twelve-year heartache is concluded by touching Jesus, so are Jairus's twelve years of joy restored by the Master's hand.

This is not a coincidence. Mark tells us the story so we can see, and so his Roman first readers could see, the linkage on display. Twelve years. Two daughters. One Christ. It is divine math, and the resulting celebrations in two lives, Jairus and the woman, ring out the joy that can be experienced only when you have been in the waiting—and the end of the waiting has brought the best of all possible solutions.

The Glory of Love

I am a sucker for a movie with a happy ending. I am always amazed at how I tear up when the third-string player hits the winning home run or the couple is finally back together or the soldier comes home to a hero's welcome. I love it. Somehow, there is something heartwarming about seeing things end up the right way— even if it is just in the world of make-believe. Real life isn't always so accommodating. The late-inning sub sometimes strikes out, the couple sometimes splits up and goes their separate ways, and the hero all too often comes home in a flag-draped coffin.

For those in the waiting, the Christmas hymn, "I Heard the Bells on Christmas Day," captures the melancholy of broken dreams and unmet expectations, saying:

> And in despair I bowed my head:
> "There is no peace on earth," I said,
> "For hate is strong and mocks the song
> Of peace on earth, good will to men."
> —*Henry Wadsworth Longfellow, 1867*

Life can be filled with cares for which no one cares but you. Yet in the face of such despair, Christ speaks words of hope. We may not always see the kind of tangible solutions that Jairus and this woman experience, but that does not diminish the caring heart of the Savior. His comfort can enter our times of waiting in ways just as substantial as the woman's healing and the child's resurrection. A love proven and displayed on a cross is not in any way negated by the harsh realities of our brokenness. Rather, His heart for us is proven all the more as He enters into our pain and joins with us in our waiting.

In many popular love songs, the singer (usually representing a forlorn teenager) would try to prove his love by describing the lengths to which he would go to prove his love. The promise? Climb any mountain, swim any ocean, endure any hardship, battle any foe. As American musician Peter Cetera sang, "We did it all for the glory of love."

Consider on that basis the glory of God's love for us, "For God so loved the world, that He gave His only begotten Son, that whoever believes in Him shall not perish, but have eternal life" (John 3:16).

Now consider on that basis the glory of Christ's love for us, "Who will separate us from the love of Christ? Will tribulation, or distress, or persecution, or famine, or nakedness, or peril, or sword?" (Romans 8:35).

The season in the waiting for Jairus and the woman exposes us to that love, which is seen in Christ's compassionate care for a woman and a girl—neither of whom would have been valued in the culture of the day—but were highly valued by Christ. And loved by Him.

A Heart That Confronts

Jesus and a Pharisee

Sometimes I feel like I'm part of an entire generation of George McFlys. George, the milquetoast dad of a suburban family in the film *Back to the Future*, has trouble at home. He has trouble with his wife. He has trouble with his kids. At work, he has trouble with his boss, the very unlikable Biff Tannen—a bully who has caused George problems since his high school days back in the 1950s. When he is challenged to stand up and do something about the abuse he had received for years, George weakly responds, "I just can't . . . stand . . . *confrontation.*"

In 1980, five years before *Back to the Future* came out, Christian counselor David Augsburger wrote a book that would challenge this fear of confrontation. In fact, he raised this concern to a level of spiritual responsibility. In *Caring Enough to Confront*, Augsburger encouraged followers of Christ to recognize that relationship carries with it responsibility—and that this responsibility is sometimes neither easy nor enjoyable.

For me, this was a fairly new idea at that time. I had derived from life experiences the mantra that if you can't say anything nice, you shouldn't say anything at all (a sentiment familiar to many of us). We chose the awkward silence of self-protection instead of the awkward moment of challenging someone. Even worse was being shown that I was wrong in my assessment of whatever it was that I thought needed confronting.

Later, however, I discovered that caring enough to confront was actually higher ground. Doing a hard thing is not the same as doing a bad thing. In fact, the Scriptures tell us, "Faithful are the wounds of a friend" (Proverbs 27:6).

The apostle Paul added his own voice to the chorus of this genuine concern when he told the churches of Galatia, "Brethren, even if anyone is caught in any trespass, you who are spiritual, restore such a one in a spirit of gentleness; each one looking to yourself, so that you too will not be tempted" (Galatians 6:1).

Yes, confrontation is to be done with gentleness (not a condemning or judgmental spirit) and with a deep sense of our own spiritual frailty (not spiritual pride or superiority)—but it *is* to be done. Sometimes confrontation is what love requires of us. If, that is, we care enough to take the risk. Care enough to expose our own vulnerability. Care enough to confront.

The challenge of confrontation is a responsibility that Jesus himself took very seriously. And in Luke 7 Jesus's caring act of confrontation will be directed at someone who clearly thinks the Galilean Rabbi's aim is off.

A Case of Opposites

Now one of the Pharisees was requesting [Jesus] to dine with him, and He entered the Pharisee's house and reclined at the table. And there was a woman in the city who was a sinner; and when she learned that He was reclining at the table in the Pharisee's house, she brought an alabaster vial of perfume, and standing behind Him at His feet, weeping, she began to wet His feet with her tears, and kept wiping them with the hair of her head, and kissing His feet and anointing them with the perfume. (Luke 7:36–38)

Whether on stage, film, or television, one of the most enduring comedy concepts of the last fifty years has been the often hilarious construct of playwright Neil Simon, *The Odd Couple*. The fastidious, neat Felix Unger is positioned in stark contrast to the slovenly, disheveled Oscar Madison. The tension generated by such opposite approaches to life made these two characters unlikely candidates for roommates—but that was what made the comedy work. Each incident was punctuated by either Felix or Oscar experiencing the frustration of engaging life with someone who clearly saw life the wrong way. And the more those opposites rubbed each other the wrong way, the funnier it was for the audience.

Not all such friction results in humor, however. In Luke 7, we are introduced to the consummate polar opposites of first-century Israel. A man versus a woman. A Pharisee versus a "sinner." A person fully aware of her spiritual poverty and another who is clueless to his spiritual need. Talk about an odd couple!

The man's name is Simon. He is described as a Pharisee, connecting this encounter to the earlier confrontation between Jesus and the Pharisees. There they turned their back on the offer of grace and wholeness (v. 30) that Jesus brought—and that the lower echelons of Jewish society happily embraced. This tension between those who were embracing Jesus's message and the religious leaders who refused it sets the stage for Simon's dinner party. As one of those described as having rejected God's purposes for themselves, he invites Jesus to his home for a meal. Jesus accepts that invitation in spite of the ongoing conflict with people just like Simon.

At events such as this one, the invited guests would recline at the table to enjoy both the meal and the conversation. Here they would have expected a dialogue with laser-like intensity between Jesus and His host. However, when traveling dignitaries or celebrities entered a home for such gatherings, men of the town—men, not women—were allowed to line the interior walls of the house to quietly listen to the conversation. So using a bit of biblical imagination, we can envision a fairly standard mealtime during Jesus's public ministry. A table spread with food, a watching crowd, and a conservative, traditional member of the religious establishment probing Jesus for flaws in His teaching.

But this is an odd *couple*—and the second person in the couple is not Jesus. In verse 37 we see a woman entering a scene where she does not belong. But not only is she a woman in the wrong place, she is also the *wrong* woman in the wrong place. Why? Because she is presented to us as "a sinner," and apparently this was a fact that was well-known in the community.

The term *sinner* doesn't refer to someone who stumbles into wrong behavior or unintentional violations of right and wrong. It is more intense, speaking of someone who has dedicated and devoted himself or herself to sin as a lifestyle. This is a strong designation, and it is generally thought to mean that she was a known prostitute in the community. Some scholars, however, speculate that she may have simply been a Gentile, outside of the covenant faith of Israel and therefore unworthy to be in such a place.

Either way, the contrast could not have been more severe: a righteous man of religion and a woman known to be a sinner. And the already controversial Jesus will be caught in the middle between them because the woman doesn't merely show up—she is on a mission.

A Scandalous Act

And there was a woman in the city who was a sinner; and when she learned that He was reclining at the table in the Pharisee's house, she brought an alabaster vial of perfume, and standing behind Him at His feet, weeping, she began to wet His feet with her tears, and kept wiping them with the hair of her head, and kissing His feet and anointing them with the perfume. Now when the Pharisee who had invited Him saw this, he said to himself, "If this man were a prophet He would know who and what sort of person this woman is who is touching Him, that she is a sinner." (Luke 7:37–39)

Sally Field won a Best Actress Oscar for her portrayal of a labor activist named Norma Rae in a movie of the same name. *Norma Rae*, somewhat based on a true story, depicted a woman trying to help unionize the textile factory where she worked. In the process, she defied the norms of her times in ways that earned her scorn and placed her in danger. Yet the inconvenient reality was that she didn't care about scorn or danger. She cared about fairness in the workplace. She cared about proper pay and treatment for workers. And she didn't care if she made others uncomfortable in the pursuit of her goals.

Now as we rewind back to Luke 7, we discover a woman who is centuries ahead of her time. This "sinful" woman is going to rattle the masculine cage of every man in that room—apart from Jesus himself. She is going to accomplish her purpose for coming, and if that makes people uncomfortable, their angst will not deter her in the slightest.

Her mission? To give honor to Jesus.

Her methods? Scandalous behavior in front of the "proper" people of the community.

What did that look like? As we have seen, it begins with her violation of social protocols and entering a men's-only event. For a woman to enter that room at that time—unless she was there to help serve the meal—would have been shocking. Who did she think she was? Violation of this testosterone-only zone would have sent shock waves throughout the community, but her motives will become abundantly clear. Her presence in the room has virtually nothing to do with who she is and everything to do with who Jesus is, for He is why she came.

As the crowd of men watch in stunned silence, she locates Jesus, who like the other invited guests, is reclining at the table (the normal posture for dining in first-century Israel). Finding Jesus in this position, however, perfectly accommodates her intentions. She comes behind Jesus and does three things—seemingly in one movement. She anoints Jesus with the highly valuable perfume she has carried into this tense space, she weeps so profusely that she is able to wash the Master's feet with her tears, and in a massive social error she lets her hair down in public and uses her hair—her glory (1 Corinthians 11:15)—to wipe and dry Jesus's feet.

The men, represented by Simon's private thoughts, weigh this heavily. Simon "said to himself, 'If this man were a prophet He would know who and what sort of person this woman is who is touching Him, that she is a sinner'" (v. 39).

Simon's private musings range in two directions. To Simon, not only does the woman prove who (or what) she is by the shameful way she is behaving but she may also be simultaneously proving who Jesus isn't. Jesus has been proclaimed a prophet, but a *real* prophet would know better. A *real* prophet would condemn her actions. A *real* prophet would hold the line of religious righteousness.

To Simon the Pharisee, everything about this is wrong. To the men around the table, everything about this is wrong. To the watching members of the community, everything about this is wrong.

The woman doesn't care. To her, scandalous though it may

seem, everything about this is right. And what will arguably shock Simon most is that Jesus seems to agree with her!

A Revealing Story

And Jesus answered him, "Simon, I have something to say to you." And he replied, "Say it, Teacher." "A moneylender had two debtors: one owed five hundred denarii, and the other fifty. When they were unable to repay, he graciously forgave them both. So which of them will love him more?" Simon answered and said, "I suppose the one whom he forgave more." And He said to him, "You have judged correctly." (Luke 7:40–43)

The Bible is full of both stories and storytellers. In the Jewish culture, story was more than a significant tool for communication, for teaching, and for entertainment. It was part of the fabric of the culture. Perhaps that is why story was also a subtle yet profound means for confrontation.

The classic example of this, of course, tracks back into the Old Testament days of David the king. His life, checkered by combat and consecration, women and worship, had severely gone off the rails. Abandoning his royal responsibility to lead Israel's armies, he lounges in the palace (2 Samuel 11) and then has a one-nighter with Bathsheba, the wife of one of his "mighty men of valor." The result of that night of passion is a pregnancy, which results in the deceit-laden murder of her husband—the faithful soldier Uriah.

Hoping to cover up his moral failure, David goes underground for about a year—until Nathan shows up. Nathan is a prophet who, in spite of the awkwardness of the situation, cares enough to confront (2 Samuel 12). And his method of choice is storytelling. A family, a ewe lamb, and a scoundrel for a neighbor are the principal characters of the story—and David responds to Nathan's tale with near-nuclear rage, essentially exposing his own scoundrel-like behavior against the slain Uriah. Through the medium of story, David was disarmed and exposed.

In the tension of the meal at Simon the Pharisee's house, Jesus resorts to this approach in order to challenge his host's attitudes and thoughts. It is a very soft approach, but make no mistake about it, the religious leader is firmly in the crosshairs of Jesus's story of the two debtors.

Much like our world, ancient Israel was a land of debt, debtors, and creditors, so the story recorded in Luke 7:40–43 would have had front-of-mind relevance for the people at the table and around the room. Present there would have been representatives of both sides of the debt equation, and no doubt most of them would have easily found their own place in Jesus's story. While the presence of debtors and a creditor in the story would have come as no surprise, the wrinkle of forgiving the debt would have been shocking.

It is helpful to remember that in that day a denarius was the equivalent of a day's wages—and money was not easy to come by (no doubt the reason for the prevalence of creditors and debtors). A debt of fifty days (almost two months') salary would be massive, but the debt of five hundred denarii was even greater—approaching two years' wages!

The key element in the story, however, is not simply the amounts owed or the disparity between them. In fact, when Jesus applies the story, the only reason to even notice the disparity of debt is to underline the power of the response of love and gratitude from the forgiven person.

The key element is that both of them are debtors. Both of them are accountable. Both of them have a need, and therein lies the problem. The woman clearly sees her need—but Simon is oblivious to his own need. *The Bible Exposition Commentary* says:

> Simon's real problem was *blindness*: he could not see himself, the woman, or the Lord Jesus. It was easy for him to say, "*She* is a sinner!" but impossible for him to say, "I am also a sinner!" (See Luke 18:9–14). Jesus proved that He was indeed a prophet by reading Simon's thoughts and revealing his needs.
>
> The parable does not deal with the *amount* of sin in a person's life but the *awareness* of that sin in his heart. How much sin must a person commit to be a sinner? Simon and the woman were both sinners. Simon was guilty of sins of the spirit, especially pride, while the woman was guilty of sins of the flesh (see 2 Corinthians 7:1). Her sins were known, while Simon's sins were hidden to everyone except God. *And both of them were bankrupt and could not pay their debt to God.* Simon was just as spiritually bankrupt as the woman, only he did not realize it.

Jesus's purpose in telling this story is to open Simon's eyes to his own deep spiritual need. Luke's purpose in including this tale is to remind the readers of the sad reality of what we were just told in verses 29–30: "When all the people and the tax collectors heard this, they acknowledged God's justice, having been baptized with the baptism of John. But the Pharisees and the lawyers rejected God's purpose for themselves."

Tragically, the evidence of their rejection of Jesus's offer of grace is lived out on the stage of life. At Simon's feast, the theoretical odd couple comes to life in flesh. A woman and a man. Both were on level ground as debtors—but they displayed very different responses to the spiritual need their personal, spiritual debt represents.

Jesus has been vilified by the religious establishment for His willingness to associate with and reach out to the notorious elements of Jewish society, but the fact that He is reclining at Simon's table should have been a reminder that the religionists were not forgotten in His mission to help and heal. He had come for all—including them. And in trying to penetrate Simon's religious armor, Jesus asks His host to make the application—a heart of love and gratitude is the normal response to forgiveness, and if you are aware of the depths of your real need, the more you will appreciate the wonder of being forgiven. For that, love is the only appropriate response.

A Striking Reality

Turning toward the woman, He said to Simon, "Do you see this woman? I entered your house; you gave Me no water for My feet, but she has wet My feet with her tears and wiped them with her hair. You gave Me no kiss; but she, since the time I came in, has not ceased to kiss My feet. You did not anoint My head with oil, but she anointed My feet with perfume. For this reason I say to you, her sins, which are many, have been forgiven, for she loved much; but he who is forgiven little, loves little." (Luke 7:44–47)

I love the intentionality of Jesus—how He did everything purposefully and with great care. That powerful idea hits me again when I read verse 44, where Luke says, "Turning toward the woman, He said to Simon . . ." Notice the physicality of the moment. Jesus is *speaking* to Simon, but He is *looking* at the woman. This woman is clearly in the spotlight, and Jesus sees her thoroughly. The question is, does Simon?

Simon sees a notorious sinner who has overstepped her bounds by coming into his house and disturbing his event. In fact, Simon thinks he *does* see her—and that he sees her far more accurately than the Rabbi Jesus did. But Jesus is probing. He is trying to awaken Simon's heart from the slumber of religious self-satisfaction and open his eyes to see grace and mercy. That is what Jesus sees.

Jesus's next words have been debated by scholars for centuries. What is Jesus saying? Is she forgiven because she washed Jesus's feet? Should Simon go and do likewise?

Based on the evidence of the New Testament, her forgiveness cannot be based on her deeds. Her deeds (weeping, washing, and wiping Jesus's feet) are the fruit of already having been forgiven. This is clearly expressed in Ephesians 2:8–10:

> For by grace you have been saved through faith; and that not of yourselves, it is the gift of God; not as a result of works, so that no one may boast. For we are His workmanship, created in Christ Jesus for good works, which God prepared beforehand so that we would walk in them.

Entering into relationship with Christ is the result of faith that comes after a person responds to God's grace (vv. 8–9). This leads to loving acts of service (v. 10) motivated by gratitude to the One who has secured our rescue.

This woman's actions spring from the reality of a forgiveness that Jesus had already granted. Forgiveness was the point of the story of the debtors. They loved because they had already been released from the burden of their debt. Luke chooses not to tell us when or where that took place for the sinful woman, but Jesus's words make it clear that at some point—perhaps in recent days—she met the Savior and in faith responded to His mercy. She was then forgiven of her sin. Her mission of honor to Christ was simply born from her release from guilt and the cleansing of a heart that had been set free. Her sobbing tears and tender love are the fruit of being forgiven—not the means by which that forgiveness has been secured.

In this event there is a critical issue that must be understood. The sinful woman's spotlight is slowly moving to the man beside Jesus. Normal hospitality of that day meant that when Jesus—Simon's special guest—arrived at the house a servant would have been dispatched to wash the Master's feet. Jesus would have received an anointing of oil to refresh Him from the weariness of the day. His host would have greeted Jesus with a ceremonial kiss.

None of those things had happened—so it seems that the woman rushed in to give Jesus the honor that His host had withheld. Common hospitality should have motivated Simon to provide these courtesies, but a greater motivation had moved this woman. Grateful love had driven her to do what the moment demanded, and she stepped into the void left by Simon's oversights.

A Powerful Result

Then He said to her, "Your sins have been forgiven." Those who were reclining at the table with Him began to say to themselves, "Who is this man who even forgives sins?" And He said to the woman, "Your faith has saved you; go in peace." (Luke 7:48–50)

Religious skeptics will sometimes argue that it is inappropriate to assert that Jesus is God because He never made that claim for himself. Simon the Pharisee could be called to the witness stand to give testimony in opposition to that claim, because as this episode winds down he listened to Jesus make a de facto claim to being God by doing what only God can do—fully absolve and forgive sins.

Although it appears that Simon understands the claim Jesus is making, the Pharisee does not acknowledge his own need of that forgiveness. I wonder how Jesus felt that day after leaving Simon's house. Was He troubled by the Pharisee's lack of self-awareness? Saddened by the man's unwillingness to embrace the reality of his need? I am convinced that the One who really could forgive Simon's sins must have felt some measure of grief over the Pharisee's intransigence.

Why? Because we easily forget that Simon was as much a part of Jesus's rescue mission as that woman or the man born blind or the leper or the woman with the bloody hemorrhage. Jesus came to seek and save the lost—and that included the Pharisee who could not come to grips with his own lostness.

We so often think of the Pharisees as the religious antagonists with whom Jesus engaged in verbal battles that we forget that they too were sheep in need of the Shepherd. And maybe that realization helps us to understand Jesus's heart behind all of those debates. He reached out to the leper with a touch and to the woman at the well with the offer of a drink of living water. The religionists required more. They needed to be confronted—and Jesus did just that.

As seen in the case of Simon the Pharisee, Jesus was doing everything necessary to present the need and the remedy to the religious leaders, and in some cases they responded. But in all cases Jesus cared, and He cared enough to confront so grace could take hold. The woman got it! Did Simon?

Sin and despair, like the sea-waves cold,
Threaten the soul with infinite loss;
Grace that is greater, yes, grace untold,
Points to the refuge, the mighty cross.

Dark is the stain that we cannot hide.
What can avail to wash it away?
Look! There is flowing a crimson tide;
Brighter than snow you may be today.

Marvelous, infinite, matchless grace,
Freely bestowed on all who believe!
You that are longing to see His face,
Will you this moment His grace receive?

Grace, grace, God's grace,
Grace that will pardon and cleanse within;
Grace, grace, God's grace,
Grace that is greater than all our sin!
                    —*Julia H. Johnston, 1910*

A Heart That Reaches
Jesus and the Canaanite Woman

When I was a pastor, I subscribed to *Leadership Journal*, a periodical dedicated to informing and encouraging men and women in ministry. The articles were often fascinating, and timely interviews with ministry leaders from around the world were insightful. To be honest, my favorite features in the *Journal* were the cartoons. Witty and a bit sardonic, they had to have been drawn by someone with a background in church work. They were spot on!

One of my favorite cartoons depicted an older gentlemen talking to a couple of kids. He had rolled up his shirtsleeve and was pointing to a pronounced scar on his bicep. He explained, "I got this one in the First Battle of Guitars in the Sanctuary back in '82." Like I said—spot on.

Even years removed from much of the overt conflict over music styles in the church, we continue to see the blowback and collateral damage in our churches from what have become known as the "worship wars." In those conflicts over both style and substance, the concept of worship has been largely relegated to music and how it is (or should be) presented when followers of Christ assemble together to "worship."

So what does worship look like? Where can it be found?

In John 4, Jesus told a Samaritan woman (see chapter 3) that the Father seeks after and desires true worshippers to worship Him (vv. 23–24). It is arguably one of the most amazing statements Jesus ever made. God is looking for and desires true worshippers—but what is it that makes someone a true worshipper? Is it any of the following?

- A certain style of music, dress, and/or liturgy?
- The proper religious heritage or denominational affiliation?
- A required volume of biblical knowledge?

What constitutes the kind of true worshipper Jesus was calling for and the Father is looking for? I think pastor and author A. W. Tozer (1897–1963) may have been on the right track. He wrote,

> What comes into our minds when we think about God is the most important thing about us.
>
> The history of mankind will probably show that no people has ever risen above its religion, and man's spiritual history will positively demonstrate that no religion has ever been greater than its idea of God. Worship is pure or base, as the worshiper entertains high or low thoughts about God.
>
> For this reason, the gravest question before the church is always God Himself, and the most portentous fact about any man is not what he at a given time may say or do, but what he in his deep heart conceives God to be like. (*The Knowledge of the Holy*, p. 9)

This is the true question of worship. Who is God and what makes Him worthy of our attention? To that end, Jesus came to our world seeking men and women He could build into true worshippers. But how did they respond?

- He came to His own and they, broadly speaking, did not receive Him (John 1:11).
- Many of His followers would stop following Him altogether after He presented a message that was particularly tough to accept (John 6:60, 66).
- The disciples failed to grasp the nature of this call to worship (Matthew 14:31).
- The religious leaders rejected the One who called out to them (Matthew 15:8–9).
- Even the closest of His disciples, Simon Peter, failed to see Him rightly (Matthew 15:16) and failed to understand the heart of worship.

The last two of those incidents are particularly significant, because they form the setup for what happens next. Upon the failure of the Jewish leaders and His own followers to grasp worship, Jesus takes radical action (Matthew 15:21). He leaves the Galilee region and goes northwest to the coastal areas of Tyre and Sidon. Tyre was thirty-five miles from Capernaum and Sidon was a fifty-mile walk. Depending upon where they were specifically going in the region, this would have been a two- to three-day walk. This is extremely important for several reasons:

- This is the only time during Jesus's public ministry that He steps out of the larger Palestine region and into strictly gentile territory.
- He was seeking to refresh himself from the increasing conflicts that surrounded Him (Mark 7:24) and to actually withdraw for a bit from the crowds that followed Him.

He retreated from the press of the crowd and the malice of His enemies and withdrew to a quiet place of solitude—and to a woman with a true heart of worship. As she comes into view (Matthew 15:22) we have a scene unlike any other in the gospels. In fact, one writer described it, saying, "There is no incident in our Lord's earthly ministry more puzzling than this." For that reason alone this encounter bears careful consideration.

An Unhappy Encounter

How does it feel when you are talking with someone and that person ignores you? How do you feel? How does that feeling change when you factor in the importance of what you are talking about? Let's take this horizontal frustration and turn it vertically—when you talk to God about things, does it ever seem as if He is ignoring you? Does that feel wonderful? I didn't think so.

In Matthew 15, a gentile woman came to Jesus with the most important request and concern you could imagine—the suffering of her daughter. Notice Matthew's account of the story: "And a Canaanite woman from that region came out and began to cry out, saying, 'Have mercy on me, Lord, Son of David; my daughter is cruelly demon-possessed'" (Matthew 15:22).

What might we be able to understand about this woman from the text? Let's start with the geographical context of her home. Tyre and Sidon were twin cities near the seashore of the Mediterranean. In the Old Testament era, this territory was occupied by Canaanites, and she is described that way ethnically (Mark 7 calls her a "Syrophoenician"). This general area had been the place from which Jezebel (1 Kings 16) had come to Israel, bringing her regional Baal worship to her marriage with King Ahab and as a result to the northern kingdom of Israel. Later the region was conquered by Alexander the Great, who imported Greek thinking, philosophy, and gods. The area was still heavily Greek in culture in the time of Jesus.

Additionally, the Syrophoenicians had historically worshipped Ashtoreth (Astarte) since the days of Elijah. Ashtoreth was the goddess of beauty who was worshipped through the absolute pursuit of pleasure, including an Epicurean lifestyle, which had a similar pursuit.

These details don't paint a particularly pretty picture. But there is one other piece of information that may play a part in our understanding of this woman and this event. In his account Mark says that as Jesus's fame grew people from all over the region were drawn to Him for help and for rescue:

> Jesus withdrew to the sea with His disciples; and a great multitude from Galilee followed; and also from Judea, and from Jerusalem, and from Idumea, and beyond the Jordan, and the vicinity of Tyre and Sidon, a great number of people heard of all that He was doing and came to Him. (Mark 3:7–8)

Why would the woman come to Jesus in the first place? Perhaps it was because she had heard the stories of His power from some of her neighbors who had traveled to the Galilee to meet Him. Now, anguished over the demonic possession that afflicted her daughter, she comes to Jesus and bares her soul to Him. "[She] began to cry out, saying, 'Have mercy on me, Lord, Son of David; my daughter is cruelly demon-possessed'" (Matthew 15:22).

When Matthew says that she "began to cry out," his words carry a sense of continuous action. She begins to and then continues to cry out over and over and over again. Imagine the scene if you can. Jesus and His men have crossed over into pagan territory and perhaps are talking together as they walk (the normal practice for a first-century rabbi and his followers) when they begin to hear shouts and screams. Not only is it unnerving but it also may have seemed rather embarrassing to the disciples to have this woman screaming at them at the top of her voice. In fact, they may have been so taken aback by her behavior that they didn't really notice her words.

She begins with a plea for mercy. The cry, "Lord, have mercy" has been described by Denver pastor Robert Gelinas as the "most-prayed prayer in the Bible." It is an acknowledgement of a person's total and absolute dependence. It is asking of the Lord what we are incapable of doing for ourselves and what we may not even deserve. In his book *The Mercy Prayer*, Gelinas presents a beautifully crafted prayer that captures the heart of "Kyrie Eleison"—which is Greek for "Lord have mercy." He wrote:

> For those who sin, and for those who suffer,
>> For those who suffer because of sin, and for those who
>> sin to alleviate suffering,
>> Lord, have mercy on us.

This prayer resonates with the cry of a desperate mom who comes to Jesus and pleads for mercy. Notice what else she does. She calls Jesus "Son of David." In ancient Israel this was a messianic term recognizing not just ethnicity or family heritage but also ascribing a higher title to the person—the sent One Israel had awaited for centuries. A chapter *before* Peter's declaration of the person of Christ at Caesarea Philippi (see Matthew 16:13–20), this gentile woman was already convinced of the true nature of the Person she was addressing.

One more thing demands our attention, and it resonates deeply with the heart of any parent. She says, "Have mercy on *me* . . ." It is her daughter who has been demon-possessed, but it is this mom who feels the weight and the burden of fear, despair, hopelessness, and anguish caused by the condition. No parent can watch his or her child suffer without entering into that suffering with the child, and this is exactly what drives this desperate mom to Jesus.

It's not surprising that this mother would feel so deeply for her daughter and want to intercede for her. What *is* shocking to us, however, is Jesus's response—or perhaps better put, Jesus's *lack* of response.

"But He did not answer her a word" (Matthew 15:23).

If we are being honest, this throws us off-balance. When Jairus came to Jesus pleading for his little girl, Jesus immediately took steps to come to her aid. Now this woman comes to Jesus to seek mercy for her little girl, and Jesus ignores her! Clearly this is not what we have come to expect as Jesus-like behavior. It almost seems as if Jesus was away and Peter had taken over for a minute. I can easily envision Peter acting this way, but Jesus? Not a chance.

To add to her pain, not only does Jesus seem to ignore her pleas but the disciples also begin a counterattack—begging Jesus to send her and her loud embarrassment away: "And His disciples came and implored Him, saying, 'Send her away, because she keeps shouting at us'" (Matthew 15:23).

Just as she has been unceasingly crying out for Jesus's help, the disciples are now unceasingly crying out for Jesus to refuse to help her and send her away. Rather than having pity on her heartache, the disciples want to send her away, further marginalizing this already marginalized woman.

This was a scene of verbal turbulence—the woman and the disciples all relentlessly crying out, and Jesus, somber as a statue, silently standing in the eye of that storm.

Being Put on Hold

One of the more frustrating experiences many of us face on a regular basis is dealing with call centers. We have a problem with our cable provider, our airline tickets, our insurance, or our computer, and we call the 800 number. After being told how important our call is to the company, we are put on hold. Sometimes we listen to music, sometimes we listen to ads—but we wait.

How do you feel when you are put on hold? How must it have felt for this woman to be put on hold by Jesus? It is one of those good news/bad news situations. The bad news is that Jesus hasn't said yes, but the good news is that He also hasn't said no. His silence forms the ultimate non-response. However, if we were troubled when Jesus ignored her cries for help, the story gets, frankly, even more disturbing when Jesus finally breaks His silence: "But He answered and said, 'I was sent only to the lost sheep of the house of Israel'" (Matthew 15:24).

Seriously? Did Jesus actually tell her He wouldn't help her because she is the wrong ethnicity? Now this *really* doesn't seem like Jesus. By the way, that cheering you hear in the background would be the disciples celebrating Jesus's rejection of this woman's request.

But why would He turn her away? Some might speculate that Jesus helped Jairus because he was an observant Jew and that He refuses this woman because she is a pagan. But how does that stand up against the earlier episode where Jesus helped the Roman soldier? This is getting more puzzling by the moment.

If, though, we had a bit of embedded video that captured the scene, I wonder if we would understand better. I wonder if perhaps there was a look on Jesus's face or a tone to Jesus's voice that told her He was not rejecting her outright. It would seem that something is inviting her in, because rather than walking away in despair, she presses the issue further: "But she came and began to bow down before Him, saying, 'Lord, help me!'" (Matthew 15:25).

The phrase we've been driving toward in this entire episode is now upon us. When the narrator (Matthew) tells us she "began to bow down before Him" he utilizes an expression used of worship. Consider the majesty of this—this woman would seem to have been ignored, rejected, and insulted by Jesus, and still she comes forward and offers her worship to Him.

This is a remarkable scene, for it is not a Torah scholar or even one of the Twelve who offers Jesus worship—it is a pagan woman from the wrong ethnic group. Her persistence is laudable and her unbending faith in Jesus is a thing of beauty. We think, *Surely now Jesus will help this woman and her daughter.* But Jesus continues to surprise with what, in print on a page, seems to be a completely out-of-character callousness.

A Humble Heart of Worship

There are some statements that seem to be constants in our day. Statements like:

- It has to get worse before it can get better.
- The cure is worse than the disease.
- You can't heal until you hurt.

Just as those platitudes leave us flat and empty, I doubt that they would have done much for this Canaanite woman either.

When we or those we love are hurting, words can be easy response devices. But they can also fall far short of the need of the moment. This woman could easily have turned her back and walked away. She has pleaded with Jesus and has been ignored.

She has been insulted by the disciples. With her broken heart, these things alone could be devastating, but Jesus's next response feels even more harsh. "And He answered and said, 'It is not good to take the children's bread and throw it to the dogs'" (Matthew 15:26).

From the perspective of a neutral observer, things only seem to have gotten worse! She has been ignored, rejected, and insulted. Now Jesus calls her a dog. What is behind that? Ancient Jews, by virtue of their distinct place as the covenant people of Israel, had a remarkably low view of other humans. Those who were gentiles were outsiders, and that sense of distance from the God of the covenant often resulted in their being referred to as dogs (see Philippians 3:2).

Even worse, however, this term was generally used to refer to street dogs—the disease-carrying, filth-laden first century equivalent of rats. It's a terrible picture to be sure, but that was a view commonly held by Jewish people of that day. In spite of that, see the woman's response to this latest verbal setback. "But she said, 'Yes, Lord; but even the dogs feed on the crumbs which fall from their masters' table'" (Matthew 15:27).

She refuses to let go! Having offered Jesus her heart, her daughter, her need, and her worship, she now offers Him her humble trust. What she had picked up on was that when Jesus used the word *dogs*, He did not suggest (as Paul would do in the Philippians 3:2 passage) a negative connotation. Rather than calling her vermin, Jesus uses an affectionate term for a beloved house pet, a puppy. It signals welcome, not rejection—and she jumps at this welcome.

It is as if she were saying, "I accept! I gladly will accept the crumbs that fall from the table, as long as it's your table in your house. I have no desire to deprive your children—just let a crumb of grace fall to help my child. I accept your invitation—and I trust you to meet our need." Jesus's response? "Then Jesus said to her, 'O woman, your faith is great; it shall be done for you as you wish.' And her daughter was healed at once" (Matthew 15:28).

Much like the Roman centurion we saw earlier (chapter 2), Jesus uses a gentile to teach His disciples the true nature of faith and in this case the worship it generates. But a question arises that cannot be ignored. Why did Jesus treat this woman the way He did if He was going to grant her request? What was the point of pulling her painfully through a series of emotional knotholes if the eventual outcome was going to be the same anyway?

I have a theory and at the heart of the theory is this: not everything that happens *to* us is *for* us. Sometimes the things we experience are actually for the benefit of others.

When I was a pastor, many times I would visit someone from our church who was hospitalized, and the medical staff would tell me that their own lives had been deeply affected in a positive way by spending time with that person. In the midst of battling a serious illness, the person from our church had been used of God to show a heart of confidence, faith, and hope that the medical personnel could not ignore. Perhaps that experience of hospitalization was not *for* my church member. Perhaps it had been *for* the benefit of those staff who, for reasons known only to them and to God, desperately needed to see what a heart for God looks like.

I am convinced that something similar has happened here. What happened *to* the woman and her daughter was *for* the disciples. They had been so long in a religious system that bought and sold worship activities that they needed a new reference point for what a heart of worship looks like. They had been exposed to Christ, but like the religious leaders they had not gotten the point.

The appropriate response to Jesus was (and is) more than just being fascinated by His teaching or impressed by His miracles. The appropriate response to the God who had come to them in flesh was humble faith and worship, and this woman had demonstrated this heart clearly.

Perhaps that is why Jesus turns His men around, and they head back to Galilee (Matthew 15:29). This was no random visit—Jesus had come for this woman and her daughter. He had walked His men two to three days to get to this woman, and now He walks them two to three days back to the Sea of Galilee. Why such a dramatic step? Because Jesus wanted His disciples to encounter a heart of worship, and to do that He reached across geographical, ethnic, religious, and cultural boundaries to help her and to teach them. Her heart of worship had reached out to Christ, and He had reached into her need.

The blended themes of humility and worship, and the response of God to such a heart are regular reminders from the Scriptures:

- "LORD, You have heard the desire of the humble; You will strengthen their heart, You will incline Your ear" (Psalm 10:17).
- "A man's pride will bring him low, but a humble spirit will obtain honor" (Proverbs 29:23).
- "Clothe yourselves with humility toward one another, for GOD IS OPPOSED TO THE PROUD, BUT GIVES GRACE TO THE HUMBLE" (1 Peter 5:5).

Clearly, the God who reaches out to us finds pleasure in a heart that humbly worships and trusts Him.

Reach Out

My favorite Motown vocal group of the 1960s was the Four Tops, and one of their biggest hits was a 1966 recording that offered hope and help. Its title? "Reach Out I'll Be There." Of vastly greater significance, the Father has reached to us by sending His Son, and Jesus has reached to us by entering into everything we face and struggle with in life.

As He reaches to us, our best response, as with this hurting woman, is to humbly give Him our worship and trust, knowing that all we give to Him He can handle for our best and for His purposes. The hymn writer could easily have been speaking of her encounter with Jesus when he penned:

> All to Jesus I surrender,
> All to Him I freely give;
> I will ever love and trust Him,
> In His presence daily live.
> All to Jesus I surrender,
> Humbly at His feet I bow;
> Worldly pleasures all forsaken,
> Take me, Jesus, take me now.
> I surrender all, I surrender all,
> All to Thee, my blessed Savior, I surrender all.
>
> *—Judson W. Van De Venter, 1896*

SEVEN

A Heart That Restores

Jesus and a Blind Man

For a number of years, I have taught an annual Bible conference for Our Daily Bread Ministries in Liverpool, England. That's not exactly a burden, as I am a massive supporter of Liverpool Football Club and a lifelong fan of the Beatles. Therefore, Liverpool is one of my favorite places to visit in the entire world. But there is another venue in Liverpool that has been a thought-provoking place to visit—the International Slavery Museum.

On the Mersey River in Liverpool is a beautiful site called Albert Dock, where The Beatles Story museum, shops, and cafes all bustle with activity and energy. But the Slavery Museum is also in that complex, and it is a much more sobering place to spend a few hours. This museum is located in Liverpool because during the days of the slave trade Liverpool, a primary shipping port, was the third corner of the slave triangle. The ships traveled from Liverpool to West Africa where they picked up a cargo of slaves. From there, the ship would travel to the Caribbean islands to take the slaves to the sugar plantations where they would be worked to death. From the Caribbean, the ships would then return to Liverpool with a cargo of sugar for use in the empire. It was a gruesome and dehumanizing business to be part of—for both the slaves and those who transported them.

Among the best-known captains of slaving ships was John

Newton. Newton came to Christ out of the slave trade. He eventually became a minister, and he heavily influenced the life of William Wilberforce, who would lead the effort to outlaw the slave trade in England. But what Newton is best known for is a song. Perhaps not just *a* song—but *the* song. "Amazing Grace" was Newton's anthem of praise to the God who had rescued him from darkness and brought him into light. As he reveled in the love of God, Newton described his forgiveness this way:

> I once was lost, but now am found,
> Was blind but now I see.

It's that second line that grabs my attention. Once spiritually blind and bringing thousands of lives to destruction, suddenly, in Christ, he could see. What does that mean? To see? What is that? In "Amazing Grace" the singer is clearly not singing about physical sight. It is something more. It is to comprehend, to understand, to get it. That is what happened to John Newton when he came to the Savior. And that is the point of the encounter Christ has in Mark 8 with, appropriately, a blind man.

To wrestle with this matter of discovery and understanding, we want to consider this episode in Mark's gospel by first working through the story itself and then understanding the point of the story before wrestling with an important question.

The Story

And they came to Bethsaida. And they brought a blind man to Jesus and implored Him to touch him. Taking the blind man by the hand, He brought him out of the village; and after spitting on his eyes and laying His hands on him, He asked him, "Do you see anything?" And he looked up and said, "I see men, for I see them like trees, walking around." Then again He laid His hands on his eyes; and he looked intently and was restored, and began to see everything clearly. And He sent him to his home, saying, "Do not even enter the village." (Mark 8:22–26)

The scene opens in the Galilean village of Bethsaida (which means "house of fish"). On the west side of the Sea of Galilee, Bethsaida was home to part of the lake's fishing industry, as well as being the hometown of Philip, one of Jesus's disciples (John 1:44). Additionally, it was a place where Jesus had accomplished several miracles, but it was a community that had failed to respond in faith to the Messiah. As a result, Jesus had pronounced judgment on this town (Matthew 11:21).

As Jesus and His disciples come to this village, the stage is set for a future event when some people would bring a friend to Jesus. While this situation was not unique, it was a bit unusual for people who came to Jesus *not* to come on their own. The leper (Mark 1), the centurion (Matthew 8), Jairus (Mark 5), and the woman with the hemorrhage (Mark 5) all came to Jesus of their own choice and under their own power. With the leper, the centurion, and Jairus, they also came declaring their own need and making their own request.

Not here. In this case, "they" (apparently friends of the blind man) brought him to Jesus, and "they" are the ones who would make the request—pleading for Jesus to heal their friend of his blindness. The blind man doesn't say a word, and though we can't read too much into that silence, it at least causes me to wonder if the blind man was not all that excited about coming to Jesus. His friends, however, have great confidence that Jesus can help him.

At this point in the story, something fascinating happens.

Without saying a word to the blind man, Jesus grabs him by the hand and forcibly drags him away from Bethsaida.

Do you have a favorite comfort food? Comfort foods, in a sense, represent our love of familiarity. We eat those things we like, are comfortable with, and enjoy. Additionally, we often get the same thing at the same restaurants because the familiarity of it all makes us feel safe. There is a sense of security in familiarity—which is why we so naturally pursue things that are already known to us.

Jesus takes this blind man by the hand and drags him away from the comfortable familiarity of Bethsaida to deal with him in private. Imagine the emotions of the blind man. The silent Stranger (to the blind man, at least) pulls him away. Away from friends in whom he has a sense of security. Away from the village, where he would have the relative comfort of familiarity, a familiarity that he no doubt had learned by feeling his way through every nook and cranny of the place until he could navigate it as if he were sighted. Jesus pulls him away from all of that, I would suggest, to force the man into a new dependence—a dependence rooted in abandonment to Christ, not in the comfortable or the familiar.

This unusual move by Jesus is followed by something even more unusual. Jesus's method of healing this blind man is anything but conventional. Jesus spits on the man's eyes! Frankly, where I come from this would be, in the very least, viewed as rude behavior. Spitting in someone's face is insulting. It is degrading. Yet Jesus spits on the man's eyes and touches him. Then He makes another unusual move. Jesus asks the man if he can see. Most of the time when Jesus worked a miracle it was presented as a *fait accompli*—a done deal. Nothing to it.

Here, Jesus asks the man for affirmation that the healing has occurred—and the man's less than promising response was, "Well, not really." The man says he can see—which at one level confirms that a miracle has been accomplished—but he cannot see clearly. He could not distinguish men from trees. The fact that he knew his sight was garbled probably indicates that he had not been born blind, because he seems to have known what a tree looked like and what men looked like. What he was seeing didn't match up.

Jesus laid hands on the man again, and his sight was perfectly and completely restored. Jesus instructed him to not return to the village (which had been judged for its absence of faith) but instead to go home—apparently to celebrate his healing with his family and friends.

That is the story. To say that it is unusual is to vastly undersell the word *unusual*. This is the only time Jesus dealt this way with a blind man. This is the only miracle Jesus ever performed in stages. It is the only time that a person's healing was not both instantaneous and complete. Why? Depending on the theological orientation of the commentator, you can find all kinds of interesting theories, including the idea that because it was getting later in His ministry Jesus's power was waning, and He just couldn't pull off miracles as easily. Or perhaps Jesus was simply having a bad day, and it required Him to make two attempts to get it right. Still others speculate that the man did not have adequate faith to secure his healing on the first try. Really?

Why did Jesus heal this blind man in this way? It must be understood that part of what makes Christ's story so remarkable is that He suffered no creative limitations. Remember, we are talking about the Creator in human form. If we look at the infinite variety of the creation, it is an indicator of the infinite creativeness of our God.

What we see manifested in the work of creation is also made visible (pardon the pun) in the great variety of methods with which Jesus healed the blind men He encountered. With the man born blind (John 9), Jesus packed his eyes with mud and sent him to the pool of Siloam to wash them out. With blind Bartimaeus, Jesus didn't touch him at all, but healed the blind man with the spoken word. Here, Jesus spits in this man's eyes then touches him. Jesus was not limited to one method of healing blind people.

Beyond the methodology of the healing, this is the only miracle Jesus performed—of any kind—where He healed in stages. Why? How about this—He did it that way because He could, showing His very personal approach to ministry.

You're at the sandwich shop or the ice cream shop or the dry cleaner, and before you is the "take a number" machine, which, while effective, is not the most personal thing in the world. You pull the tab and wait until your number is called. But it isn't just your number—it can even feel as if *you* are the number. Do you ever feel like a number? Do you ever feel like a face in a crowd? Do you ever feel that people no longer see you?

Likewise, do you ever feel like a face in the crowd with God, or instead do you sense how personally and individually He loves you? I look at the incident with this blind man (and the other blind men as well) and see a God who is creative, intimate, and personal. For this blind man, I suspect he couldn't care less about the method itself—or if there was even a method at all. This formerly blind man could proclaim the words that John Newton would make a part of his song many hundreds of years later: "I was blind but now I see."

The Point

A few years ago, a fad of sorts started in the United States wherein people were challenged to perform "random acts of kindness." In the fast-food drive-through line, you pay for the meal of the car behind you. At the grocery store, you slip some money to a person who doesn't have enough to pay for her bags of food. On the street, you take a street person for a meal and buy him warm clothes. At a sit-down restaurant, you pick up the tab for an elderly couple. Random.

Sometimes life seems like a disconnected series of unrelated events. Sometimes it even seems that God operates with the same randomness that so often appears to characterize life. This can even seem to be the case when we look at the Scriptures.

But as Soren Kierkegaard rightly said, "Life can only be understood backwards; but it must be lived forwards." And that is true as we reflect on the events of Mark 8 and Jesus's healing of a blind man. The man is brought to Jesus by friends in what could easily be seen as a chance meeting—but was it chance? Or was it more?

There was, in fact, marvelous purpose in Jesus's work. To see that, we need to peel back the proverbial layers of this particular biblical onion. Scholars suggest that this miracle caps off a double cycle of miraculous events. Notice how these events play out:

Cycle One:
Feeding of the 5,000 (Mark 6:35–44)
Debate with Pharisees and Scribes (Mark 7:1–16)
Healing of a deaf man (Mark 7:31–37)

This is fascinating. In the miracle of abundant food, Jesus clearly feeds a multitude (Mark 6:44 says it contained 5,000 men, so it is likely that the crowd would have 15,000 or more once women and children were added in) using some bread and fish from a boy's small lunch (see John 6). This is followed by the debate in which the religionists specifically ask why Jesus and His followers eat *bread* with unwashed hands. Jesus responds by quoting Isaiah the prophet, who said their lips (Mark 7:6) betray their lack of true and living faith.

This cycle of miracles concludes with Jesus healing a person who could neither hear nor talk. Much like the blind man we have been considering, this healing was done uniquely. Once again, the healing involves spitting (Mark 7:33), and the man's hearing is restored and his speech is clarified. Bread. Lips. Speech. Though other events transpire in the midst of all this, there can be no doubt that these are links in a chain—not only are they linked to one another but they are also linked to the second cycle of miracles yet to come.

Cycle Two:
Feeding of the 4,000 (Mark 8:1–9)
Debate with the Pharisees (Mark 8:10–12)
Healing of the Blind Man (Mark 8:22–26)

The same pattern is repeated. Feeding. Debate. Healing. In the miraculous feeding, Jesus again creates abundance out of a pittance. In the debate, once again, the religious leaders attack Jesus's credibility, demanding a sign to validate His claim to a prophetic role. What is fascinating is that everything Jesus has done in these cycles of events should have been more than sufficient to prove His identity and affirm His ministry. The reasonability of that claim is found in the words of Nicodemus, the lead teacher of Israel, who addressed Jesus this way, "Rabbi, we know that You have come from God as a teacher; for no one can do these signs that You do unless God is with him" (John 3:2). Unquestionably, the evidence is there to be seen—even though the group of Pharisees in Mark 8 demands further proof.

This cycle is once again concluded with a miracle—the healing of the blind man. What is significant is that these two miracles—healing the deaf man and healing the blind man—appear only in

Mark's gospel. And they appear in Mark's record with tremendous intentionality.

What was the intent behind this? It would be naïve to say that Jesus was disinterested in the need of this blind man. Certainly, there was a clear desire to help this man. But there is also an even higher purpose: Responding to the demand that Jesus should give a sign to reveal His identity. These cycles of ministry are intended to do exactly that.

Even further, these events were designed to teach the disciples in anticipation of Caesarea Philippi. Notice how verses 27 through 29 of Mark 8 follow the healing of the blind man:

> Jesus went out, along with His disciples, to the villages of Caesarea Philippi; and on the way He questioned His disciples, saying to them, "Who do people say that I am?" They told Him, saying, "John the Baptist; and others say Elijah; but others, one of the prophets." And He continued by questioning them, "But who do you say that I am?" Peter answered and said to Him, "You are the Christ."

At Caesarea Philippi (recorded more fully in Matthew 16), Jesus would ask His disciples to declare their understanding of His identity, and these events have purposefully pointed them to His messianic role—affirmed by Peter calling Jesus "Christ," the Greek equivalent of the Hebrew word for *messiah*.

Why, then, did Jesus use these particular events to prepare the disciples for the questions He would ask? Because even lowly fishermen and laborers spent their childhood being taught the Scriptures, including the ancient prophecies about Messiah. One of the widely used Old Testament texts to point to what Messiah would be like—and how to recognize Him when He arrived—was found in Isaiah 35:4–5:

> Say to those who are fearful-hearted, "Be strong, do not fear! Behold, your God will come with vengeance, with the recompense of God; He will come and save you. Then the eyes of the blind shall be opened, and the ears of the deaf shall be unstopped." (NKJV)

The eyes of the blind have been opened (Mark 8:22–26) and the ears of the deaf have been unstopped (Mark 7:32–37). Messianic work is being done, as promised by the prophets, and that can mean only one thing—the long-awaited Messiah has arrived.

Yes, these two cycles of ministry were intended to help the hurting and to meet needs. But they were also designed to prepare the disciples for what was coming. The event at Caesarea Philippi forms a pivot-point in Jesus's ministry. The first eighteen months or so, Jesus was teaching the multitudes, performing miracles, and presenting His messianic credentials. That all changes following Caesarea Philippi. From this time forward, Jesus's ministry will be primarily (though not exclusively) focused on preparing the disciples for what was coming—the cross and the resurrection. Notice Mark 8:30–31:

> And He warned them to tell no one about Him. And He began to teach them that the Son of Man must suffer many things and be rejected by the elders and the chief priests and the scribes, and be killed, and after three days rise again.

"He began to teach them . . ." Until Caesarea Philippi, the

emphasis was on providing evidence of Jesus's identity, and nowhere is this more clear than in these two cycles of miracles. But going forward the emphasis will be on preparing for the events of the Passion. Now that they know with certainty who Jesus is, it is time for them to understand why He came. There is no randomness in this whatsoever. These events have been carefully designed.

The Question

Do you ever look at those Magic Eye pictures in the Sunday comics (a question for those who still get an actual newspaper)? If not, these are pictures that at first glance look like just a smear of color with no rhyme, reason, or meaning. But what is needed is more than a glance. You have to look . . . and then look some more. The more you look, the more clearly you see. After an extended time of focused observation, a picture begins to emerge from that mass of color. Then the picture becomes fully clear. Finally, once the picture has become clear, you can't *not* see it (please excuse the double negative). As you gaze at the colors, it is unquestionably a clear picture—and you can see it.

Similarly, for people of Jesus's generation, Jesus wasn't all that easy to figure out. What were they seeing? A wonder-worker? A prophet? A charlatan? The Messiah? The more they looked at the evidence of His works and His heart, the clearer the picture became. Those closest to Him saw Him as the Christ.

Just as it was not enough for the disciples to answer what others thought about Jesus, it is not enough for us to acknowledge the assertions of the Twelve. What do we see? What do I see? What do you see?

The evidence of the Scriptures is substantial that Jesus is exactly who they thought He was—the Christ, the Son of the living God. The existence of the church, having been birthed out of followers of Jesus who were so fearful at His crucifixion that they abandoned Him to His fate and hid from the religious authorities, bears shocking witness to His calling and power. The testimony of millions of Christ-followers over the span of two millennia underlines the claims of Scripture that the rescuing Savior is still very much alive and as much at work in our generation as He was in His own era.

What do you see? Who do you say that He is?

Open My Eyes

Some of the best stories ever written are great because they have threads of different stories that eventually converge to bring fulfillment and power to the tale.

James Michener's *Centennial,* in an opening section, converges the stories of Our People (the Arapaho of the Great Plains), the European based community of St. Louis with its merchants and markets, and the French-Canadian trapper/trader Pasquinel—who becomes a bridge between those two very different worlds.

This is nothing new. In the pages of the Bible we see the great story (God coming to the rescue of a broken world) supported by the smaller stories (individuals, ideas, events) that carry textures of story within themselves. In the healing of the blind man and the events that lead up to it, we see multiple layers of God at work:

> Judgment on Bethsaida.
> Help for the blind man.
> Lesson for the disciples.
> A parable for us.

As was true with the blind man, these events can move us from darkness to dim light and from unclear sight to a full and clear vision of the picture these events are painting. It is a portrait of the Christ—and He is ever and always the One we need to see. As hymn writer Clara Scott put it:

> Open my eyes, that I may see
> Glimpses of truth thou hast for me.
> Place in my hands the wonderful key
> That shall unclasp and set me free.
> Silently now I wait for thee,
> Ready, my God, thy will to see.
> Open my eyes, illumine me, Spirit divine!
> —*Clara Scott, 1895*

A Heart That Comforts

Jesus and a Hurting Dad

Popular culture has inflicted some pretty severe damage on the image of dads over the course of my lifetime. In the 1950s and 1960s, we had shows like *My Three Sons*, *Leave It to Beaver*, and the iconic *Father Knows Best*. In my wildest imagination, I cannot see any contemporary television outlet—cable or broadcast—that would approve a program called *Father Knows Best* today. The portrait of the fathers in those programs was consistently characterized by high morality, deep caring, and loving wisdom.

In the 1970s we had Howard Cunningham, the lovable but sadly inept dad on *Happy Days*, and the angry bigot Archie Bunker on *All in the Family*. With these and other programs, the image of fatherhood began to turn to show dads as more than flawed. They became bumbling or hateful, and they were used less and less as examples of good role models.

In the 1990s, popular culture gave us Homer Simpson and *American Dad*—presentations of fathers that are such extreme caricatures that they can only be presented in animation. The cultural depiction of dads had become a sad reflection of the overall perspective of generations of people who appeared to see dads, at best, as a necessary evil.

Now, I fully understand that in this world there are far too many poor fathers. There are abusive, mean-spirited, demanding, hurtful, emotionally distant men who severely damage children (and wives) under the authority of their title of "head of the household." I don't want to minimize the pain of anyone who has had that dark background in his or her story.

At the same time, however, I am convinced that there are lots of men trying to do it right. These are men who sacrifice themselves for the welfare or wishes of their children—men who are overwhelmed by the demands of the role of fatherhood but who are doing their best. That would be the image of fatherhood presented by the film *Cinderella Man*, which was directed by Ron Howard.

James J. Braddock, the real-life Cinderella Man, was a highly successful boxer who lost everything in the stock market crash of 1929. He entered the Great Depression desperate to support his family and keep them intact through some of the harshest moments in American history. In the film, the critical moment comes when, having seen his children shipped off because the heat has been turned off in their cellar apartment, Braddock takes the long trip to Madison Square Garden in New York City.

The Garden was the boxing capital of the world and the site of many of Braddock's previous successes. Now he is forced to go into the club at the Garden, inhabited by sportswriters and boxing aficionados who are largely untouched by the ravages of the Depression. With hat literally in hand, Braddock, the once-proud champion, begs for money from these men. The humiliation drives him to tears as he seeks the money necessary to keep his family in one piece.

That is more like the imagery of fatherhood I would like us to consider as we once again look to the heart of Christ. In Mark 9 Jesus is going to encounter a devastated father in a story about two sons. But this is also about a grieving dad who was willing to beg because of his love for his son. It is that voice—that begging, pleading voice—that we want to hear in the midst of a setting that is almost parabolic in nature.

A Moment of Awe

In a once-popular gospel song, Dottie Rambo sang about not living on a mountain but instead living in a valley chosen by the Lord. The imagery of that song rides along comfortably with the thought of Moses on the mountain in the presence of God, and Moses and Elijah on the mountaintop with Jesus. The picture is one of communion and fellowship of an almost otherworldly grace and beauty when we are "on the mountaintop." However, this brief glorious moment is eventually overtaken as life brings us down to the darkness of the valley.

This is more than a spiritual metaphor for life in a fallen world. It is also the precise scenario we come upon when we enter Mark 9.

> And Jesus was saying to them, "Truly I say to you, there are some of those who are standing here who will not taste death until they see the kingdom of God after it has come with power." Six days later, Jesus took with Him Peter and James and John, and brought them up on a high mountain by themselves. And He was transfigured before them; and His garments became radiant and exceedingly white, as no launderer on earth can whiten them. Elijah appeared to them along with Moses; and they were talking with Jesus. Peter said to Jesus, "Rabbi, it is good for us to be here; let us make three tabernacles, one for You, and one for Moses, and one for Elijah." For he did not know what to answer; for they became terrified. Then a cloud formed, overshadowing them, and a voice came out of the cloud, "This is My beloved Son, listen to Him!" All at once they

looked around and saw no one with them anymore, except
Jesus alone. As they were coming down from the mountain, He gave them orders not to relate to anyone what
they had seen, until the Son of Man rose from the dead.
(Mark 9:1–9)

Notice that the story begins on what we call the Mount of
Transfiguration where Jesus is in the presence of His Father—
radiating with glory. In that moment of wonder on the mountain,
the Father declares His love for the Son and affirms Jesus's priority
and mission. Moses and Elijah appear and engage in discussion
with Jesus about His coming work of rescue for the world (Luke
9:30–31). The glory of the mountain is so tangible that later, when
Jesus appears in the valley below, the crowd (v. 15) is amazed at
Him! Perhaps Jesus's revealed glory continued to shine in an after-
glow of that moment of awe on the mountain when His brilliant
wonder was revealed. But unlike Moses, who wore a veil because
his faced showed the radiance of the *reflected* glory of God (Exodus
34:33–35), this glory was the actual *essence* of the Son of God himself, who had been in the presence of His perfect Father.

When Jesus and His inner circle of disciples (Peter, James, John)
leave the mountaintop, however, a very different story unfolds in
the valley below—and it too is the story of a father and son. While
the event on the mount was clothed in glory, the scene below is
painted with the dark colors of oppression, fear, and failure.

Notice the contrasts between the relationships of two fathers
and their two sons. One is rooted in light; the other in darkness.
One is enriched by the presence of God; the other is tormented
by the demonic. One is reciprocal; while the other seems to be
one-directional. One is marked by joy and affirmation; the other
by pain and grief. One is characterized by utter fulfillment; the

other by abject despair. One is marked by perfection; the other by brokenness.

The contrasts become a lived-out parable that puts on display the metaphor of the difference between mountaintop and valley. The relationship on the mountaintop is perfect and without any sense of the disappointment our brokenness often produces. The relationship of the father and son in the valley carries with it the characteristics that make our broken world broken: despair, heartache, pain, fear, failure.

Two fathers. Two sons. And their stories come together in the valley—*not* on the mountaintop.

A Painful Failure

When I was a kid, my dad had a way of instructing us about things that seemed to make everything we engaged in a matter of family honor. When we succeeded, it reflected well on our family name. When we did poorly (or behaved incorrectly) it reflected badly on parents, family, and name.

This concept of shame versus honor is much more familiar to Eastern cultures than to Western society. In the West, our identity as individuals is more important to us than our place in the collective. In Eastern cultures, however, the collective is everything.

Knowing our place in the larger group—family, community, nation—is of absolute importance. Riding along with that importance is the simple fact that what we do and how we do it, as my dad poured into us, reflects on the group. It is much more than personal. It is an interrelated, interpersonal, interdependent worldview that drives the way life is lived.

Remember, then, that first-century Israel was an Eastern culture where shame and honor were significant realities. In this light we enter the valley with Jesus and His three core followers—and find all of the group, especially Jesus, dishonored by the failure of some.

> When they came back to the disciples, they saw a large crowd around them, and some scribes arguing with them. Immediately, when the entire crowd saw Him, they were amazed and began running up to greet Him. And He asked them, "What are you discussing with them?" And one of the crowd answered Him, "Teacher, I brought You my son, possessed with a spirit which makes him mute; and whenever it seizes him, it slams him to the ground and he foams at the mouth, and grinds his teeth and stiffens out. I told Your disciples to cast it out, and they could not do it." (Mark 9:14–18)

The key factor in the disciples' failure to deliver the demon-possessed boy is that they had done this before. In Mark 6:7, we read: "And He summoned the twelve and began to send them out in pairs, and gave them authority over the unclean spirits."

Not only had they been equipped for that task but they also had succeeded at it! Mark 6:12–13 gives the report of their activity. "They went out and preached that men should repent. And they were casting out many demons and were anointing with oil many sick people and healing them."

They had been commissioned to rescue demoniacs and equipped to do so, but they had failed in that very thing. What is the result of their failure? They are directly connected to Jesus by the man whose son they couldn't heal. The crowd seems to make the same link, apparently causing the verbal sparring match with the scribes. The result is that the disciples' failure is laid at Jesus's feet as if He himself had authored the disappointment the hurting dad now felt. But if their failure grieved the heartbroken father, he was not alone. Jesus also responds with a disappointment not unlike that of the dad, expressing His grief with both soliloquy and authority: "And He answered them and said, 'O unbelieving generation, how long shall I be with you? How long shall I put up with you? Bring him to Me!'" (Mark 9:19).

Who is "them"? Who is the unbelieving generation to which Jesus responds? Is it the crowd? The religious leaders? The disciples? The man and his son? Mark doesn't tell us. What he does tell us is that Jesus was distressed at the situation—and His lament is the fruit of that distress.

The resolution of the heart-cry of this hurting dad was completely in Jesus's hands—and His first step toward that resolution was, surprisingly, not to help the son. He begins by comforting the father in his pain.

An Overlooked Pain

As my father's health deteriorated, he endured almost twenty years of cardiovascular problems. Starting with his first heart attack in 1962, my dad endured a life of limitation and almost constant struggle. Especially toward the end, when he would have multiple mini-strokes a day, his suffering was so overwhelming it seemed he was the absolute center of our universe. Everyone did all they could do to ease the struggle he faced hour by hour.

That is as it should have been—but in the shadows, often just out of sight, someone else was suffering. Largely unnoticed, my mom felt the pain of every heart episode, the fear of every stroke, and the desperation of my father's ever-increasing debilitation.

Sometimes when I looked up I would see her off to the side, maybe just in the shadows, agonizing over the never-ending threat of losing her husband. Agonizing as she felt in her own chest the pain of each seizure. Agonizing as she fearfully contemplated life without her other half. Her suffering was in some ways even more difficult than my dad's, because it often went unnoticed and as a result uncared for.

As I try to visualize the scene in Mark 9, my imagination paints a similar picture. When the demonic spirit attacks, the boy is the focus of attention—for some with disgust, for others with terror, and for still others with fascination. Regardless of your point of interest, like a multi-car wreck in a NASCAR race, you can't stand to look—but you can't look away.

And in the midst of it all, this dad, much like my mom, gets lost in the shuffle of the spotlight shining on the horrific condition of his child. Yet suffer he did. Any decent parent would gladly take pain and suffering on themselves rather than to see it inflicted on their children. Like Jairus in Mark 5, this dad knows that there is no circumstance in life more painful than watching your child suffer while knowing there is nothing you can do to relieve that pain. It is a pain that is unleashed when Jesus calls for the boy to be brought to Him.

> And He answered them and said, "O unbelieving generation, how long shall I be with you? How long shall I put up with you? Bring him to Me!" They brought the boy to Him. When he saw Him, immediately the spirit threw him into a convulsion, and falling to the ground, he began rolling around and foaming at the mouth. And He asked his father, "How long has this been happening to him?" And he said, "From childhood. It has often thrown him both into the fire and into the water to destroy him. But if You can do anything, take pity on us and help us!" (Mark 9:19–22)

In other New Testament texts, both in the Gospels and Acts, we are given vivid portrayals of what the suffering of a demon-possessed person looked like. As the demon seizes this boy, the child suddenly begins to writhe in agony and cry out in anguish. For people of that generation, it was an all-too-familiar scene. The crowd can't take their eyes off the spectacle at hand. Jesus, however, while not ignoring the pain of the child, focuses on the pain of the father.

Jesus begins to pull the pain out of the dad like drawing poison from a wound. Gently asking questions, He allows this father to fully express the experience of shared suffering he has had with his boy (Luke tells us that the man describes the child as his "one and only son"—the same way that Jesus, the one and only Son of the Father is described in the Gospels). It is an experience that is drastically different from the shared glory Jesus had known with His Father.

Jesus locks in on this dad because with Jesus no one's pain is hidden in the shadows and ignored. No one is ever lost in the crowd. Jesus's care for this man is deeply personal as He tugs out of this dad's broken heart the years of hurt and helplessness he has known since the birth of this, his one and only son.

The love of Christ for hurting people is not only characteristic of His incarnational ministry but it also continues even today as He intercedes for us and as He represents us before the Father. That representation is so complete that He advocates for us when we sin and intercedes for us when we hurt (Hebrews 7:25; 1 John 2:1). None of our pain is hidden from Him and His care, and neither was the pain of the hurting father who unpacks for Jesus the struggles he and his son have endured together.

An Honest Faith

How many times a day do we put our faith in something—anything? We eat at a restaurant—an act of faith that the servers will deliver what they promise with full and undiminished adherence to health laws. We go to the doctor and trust that he or she will know what is wrong and how to deal with it—and that we will be told the truth about it.

Throughout the course of any given day, we act out thousands of tiny expressions of faith, usually with very little information to support that faith and without any way to test the person or entity in question and determine if that source is truly worthy of our trust. Nevertheless, our faith is seen as genuine—be it great or small—because we have willfully acted on it.

For all believers who have been devastated by being told that their unanswered prayers or unhealed illnesses or unsaved loved ones are due to a lack of faith on their part, it is as refreshing as a soft breeze on a warm day to find how different the heart of Jesus is. Not only is He not going to punish us for our lack of faith but He also recognizes the reality of the little faith we have—and He fully engages us anyway.

As Jesus deals one-on-one with the father of the demon-possessed boy in Mark 9, we find a man whose faith is imperfect—like ours; whose confidence in Christ is incomplete—like ours; whose spiritual frailty is real—like ours. And Jesus comes to His aid.

> And He asked his father, "How long has this been happening to him?" And he said, "From childhood. It has often thrown him both into the fire and into the water to destroy him. But if You can do anything, take pity on us and help us!" And Jesus said to him, "'If You can?' All things are possible to him who believes." Immediately the boy's father cried out and said, "I do believe; help my unbelief." (Mark 9:21–24)

The man's statement has to be understood in contrast to the heart of our friend, the leper, whom we encountered in chapter one. The leper said to Jesus, "If You are willing, You can." This poor, overwhelmed dad says, "If You can, will You?" His faith is fragile, yet he has already exhibited some measure of faith by bringing the boy to Jesus in the first place. Now the very faith that had driven the man to Jesus has been tested to the breaking point by the failure of the disciples.

In that context it is as if the man were saying to Jesus, "Your disciples couldn't do it. Can You? If You can, will You?" His plea is laced with intense emotion. He begs Jesus to have pity—care, concern, compassion—and help this hurting father with his struggling faith. What is so lovely in Jesus's response is that He never questions the size or amount of the man's faith. He simply asks the man to affirm the reality of it. The point the Master is driving for is the reality of that faith and where it is placed. That is the larger issue.

Upon hearing Jesus's words, this father breaks. His words "I do believe; help my unbelief" could be the chorus to many of our lifesongs. I deeply love the honesty and integrity of those words. Yes, the man does affirm his faith in Jesus, but he also refuses to paint that faith to seem bigger or better than it actually is. He acknowledges that not only does he need Jesus's help to heal his boy but this man also admits that he needs Jesus's help just to trust Him to heal His boy!

In these short verses, the desperate dad has made a pilgrimage of faith all on his own. Notice:

- In verse 17, his desire is for Jesus to help the boy.
- In verse 22, his request is for Jesus to help both himself *and* the boy.
- In verse 24, his request is simply for Jesus to help *him*.

This man's journey toward faith echoes the heart and spirit of the old spiritual that declared:

> Not my sister, not my brother
> But it's me, oh Lord
> Standing in the need of prayer.

This unnamed dad recognizes that he needs the help of Christ even to be able to significantly trust in Him, and his admission of absolute helplessness is all that is required. Jesus's words "All things are possible . . ." open the door to the capabilities of the divine. But as we must always remember when we pray, part of trusting God is trusting Him with the outcomes. Faith is not primarily about outcomes; it is primarily about relationship with Christ. When we trust Him with our needs, we also must trust Him with His purposes. In this case the purposes of Jesus are to provide rescue for this suffering family.

> When Jesus saw that a crowd was rapidly gathering, He rebuked the unclean spirit, saying to it, "You deaf and mute spirit, I command you, come out of him and do not enter him again." After crying out and throwing him into terrible convulsions, it came out; and the boy became so much like a corpse that most of them said, "He is dead!" But Jesus took him by the hand and raised him; and he got up. (Mark 9:25–27)

The deliverance of this boy from his demonic oppression was Jesus's answer to the father's prayer—and yet one more indication of His power over all enemies and His compassion for the victims of those enemies. After the father's emotional tug-of-war, the boy's rescue almost feels incidental. Yet the gentleness of Jesus is clearly seen as He raises the boy up and lovingly gives him back to his dad. Both father and son are now whole. The father's faith has been strengthened and purified as the son has been brought back from a living death. The Lord of light is again and ever victorious over the powers of darkness.

A Father's Story

Field of Dreams, one of the best baseball movies ever made, is not a movie just about baseball—it is also about fathers and sons. It is about how breakdowns in those relationships often leave scars of hurt, disappointment, or despair. And it is about hope and redemption and restoration to broken hearts and hurting families.

Mark 9 is a story about two sons and two fathers—and it has something to say to us whether we were loved and cared for by our fathers, or ignored and rejected by them. It reminds us that we have a Savior who, from the heart of His Father, deeply cares for our hurts and our struggles. Mark 9 is a lived-out parable of the thoroughness of that divine care:

- Jesus cared for the disciples by rescuing them from their failure.
- Jesus cared for the father by reaching into his heart and pulling him from the shadows of his pain.
- Jesus cared for the boy by rescuing him from his oppression.

How does He care for us? For me? How can I know He cares when I don't seem to see answers or have cause for hope? What is the evidence I can trust that even when I suffer and don't know why, He loves me and cares for me in my hurt and pain?

Sometimes we look for the answers to those questions in the

immediacy of the moment. At others, we look backwards into the rearview mirror of experience or forward through the telescope of expectation to find rays of hope to focus on in our desperate moments. But that is not where the true and better answer may be found. The answer to how Jesus cares for us, how Jesus loves us, and how Jesus rescues us in our struggles and sufferings and strife is ever and always this: the cross.

The proof of His care and His love and His compassion is His willingness to die for us. And no life-circumstance, daily battle, or chronic struggle can diminish the reality that His love drove Him to the cross to resolve our greatest problem—alienation from our Creator—with a remedy that will eventually take care of all the rest of our pain in an eternity of wholeness with Him.

Contemplating that eternity, John wrote:

> And I heard a loud voice from the throne, saying, "Behold, the tabernacle of God is among men, and He will dwell among them, and they shall be His people, and God Himself will be among them, and He will wipe away every tear from their eyes; and there will no longer be any death; there will no longer be any mourning, or crying, or pain; the first things have passed away." And He who sits on the throne said, "Behold, I am making all things new." (Revelation 21:3–5)

That ultimate hope can often give us the courage to endure the pressures and pains of the moment. In the meantime, there is a question that regularly falls from the lips of followers of Christ: "Does Jesus care about me and my challenges?"

This is not a new question. The disciples asked the question when the storm raged on the Galilee. Martha asked it when Mary left her alone with the task of caring for their guests. We ask it when a diagnosis is unwelcome, when a job is lost, when our prayers seem to go unanswered, and when our belief feels more like unbelief. We ask it even when we feel certain there is no one there to hear it or respond. Does Jesus care? In response to that almost timeless question, one songwriter gave his answer, and it resonates deeply with the heart of the hurting dad and rescued son of Mark 9.

> Does Jesus care when my heart is pained
> Too deeply for mirth and song;
> As the burdens press, and the cares distress,
> And the way grows weary and long?
> O yes, He cares—I know He cares!
> His heart is touched with my grief;
> When the days are weary, the long nights dreary,
> I know my Savior cares.
> —*Frank E. Graeff, 1901*

A Heart That Transforms
Jesus and a Tax Collector

We live in a world that is deeply polarized. This polarization occurs on a number of levels, with people taking sides over race, gender, politics, work, and neighborhoods. The seemingly endless list moves forward from there. In a day filled with bias and bigotry, it sometimes feels as if we are only one small step away from fully venting our sense of position and entitlement against those who just don't measure up to our standards of acceptability.

The words *measure up* scream at us from the page, because we tend to evaluate people based on a standard that we have established in our own minds. "Measuring up," however, takes on a deeper meaning when considering Randy Newman's hit song from his 1977 album *Little Criminals*. The song, entitled "Short People," exposes our tendency to label, devalue, and categorize people by absurdly talking about their height. Instead of talking about something substantial that might contribute to our own hurts and dissatisfaction with life, Newman sings about judging people according to their physical stature.

Talk about a bolt from the blue! Most of us would acknowledge that people who are vertically challenged (like my wife) haven't done anything wrong. They're just short. Yet the song treats a lack of height in the same way we might wrongly view someone's ethnicity or political affiliation. As a result, painting in the somber colors and difficult hues of prejudice, Newman's parody concludes that short people "got no reason to live." That view resonates with the history of humanity's dealings with people they might not like for arbitrary and unfair reasons.

It seems that in every culture there is some kind of system whereby people are put into categories. The haves vs. the have-nots. The good vs. the bad. The in vs. the out. The high vs. the low. The deserving vs. the undeserving. Us vs. them. These value judgments about other human beings can be destructive and are often expressive of a warped self-view.

People in first-century Israel were no different—only their categories were the righteous versus the sinners. The lawkeepers vs. the lawbreakers. It is this set of perceptions that Jesus will challenge head-on as He encounters one of the outsiders of His generation—a tax collector. Oh, and it just so happens that this particular tax collector is short. For his story, we turn to Luke 19.

A Polarized Community

"[Jesus] entered Jericho and was passing through." (Luke 19:1)

As Luke 19 opens, Jesus takes His final journey to Jerusalem, with the awaiting cross looming ever-larger on the horizon (see Luke 18:31–34). As He and His disciples make their way, they pass through the ancient city of Jericho. On the outskirts of town a blind beggar (Mark tells us his name is Bartimaeus, or son of Timaeus) asks for and receives healing from Jesus. Then Jesus and His followers enter the city.

Jericho was a fairly substantial community in the first century, with some scholars estimating a population of as much as 100,000. Why would this town be so substantial? It was situated in the Jordan River valley and controlled the river crossings as well as the Jericho Road that led to Jerusalem. As a major crossroads to the east of the capital, Jericho had become a place of substantial wealth and a highway of commerce. In addition, the fertile soil of the Jordan Valley made the region highly productive for farming.

In even more ancient times, the God of Israel had given the city of Jericho to Joshua, who destroyed it and placed a curse on anyone who rebuilt it (Joshua 6:26). But in the days of Ahab the city was rebuilt, and later Marc Antony gave Jericho to Cleopatra as a gift—beautifying the oasis community with palm trees and rose gardens. Finally, Herod enlarged the city's profile by building a winter palace, a theater, and a hippodrome. He turned Jericho into something of a leading resort community for the wealthy. This was the city of Jericho that Jesus entered in Luke 19.

Normally, we wouldn't be terribly enthralled with such seemingly peripheral details, but here they are anything but peripheral. By being a center of commerce, transportation, and agriculture, Jericho and its environs would have also been fertile ground for another industry—tax collecting. It is this confluence of circumstances that sets the stage for this encounter. Jesus and the Twelve are entering a city some have described as the Las Vegas of first-century Israel. And it was there that the Lord would encounter Zaccheus.

An Ironic Man

And there was a man called by the name of Zaccheus; he was a chief tax collector and he was rich. (Luke 19:2)

The brevity of Luke's description of Zaccheus is compounded by the fact that only Luke records this incident. Later, he will tell us (v. 3) that Zaccheus was "small in stature," but for now there are enough problems to deal with regarding this man. He is portrayed as being a tax collector; therefore, he was considered to be rich.

Tax Collectors. At its heart, tax collecting was collaboration with the occupying Roman government and forces. Like all governments, Rome craved the mother's milk of revenues and demanded that the lands it conquered pay the freight for the empire. Local collaborators (sometimes referred to as "publicans") were given tax quotas that they had to generate from the local citizens and businesses. If that weren't bad enough, tax collectors were allowed to extort as much money from the people as they could—keeping the difference for themselves. Rome happily closed its eyes to the defrauding and dishonest practices of its tax collectors as long as the empire received its imperial revenues.

Rich. The way for a tax collector to get rich was to continually overcharge people on the taxes they owed. As a result, the Jews hated these men because they represented the despised Roman conquerors and because they took advantage of their own people financially. Subsequently, these publicans were banned from worship and hated as some of the lowest life forms of their day. The Talmud even went so far as to say that although honesty and integrity were the expectations of Moses's law, there were three kinds of people to whom you could legitimately lie: thieves, murderers, and, yes, tax collectors.

This simple description of Zaccheus opens a window of understanding for us, portraying a man who was despised by his community and excluded from the faith of his fathers. He was just as fully an outcast as the leper of Mark 1—but Zaccheus's exclusion from community and synagogue life would have been seen as infinitely worse because he had chosen this line of work. The leper was a victim. Zaccheus was a volunteer.

As someone who was excluded from ceremonial life, Zaccheus would have been banned from the temple, which explains why, in the story Jesus told in Luke 18:10–14 of the Pharisee and the publican, it is the tax collector who longs to worship God. However, he is excluded and must stand "some distance away." His repentant heart longed to be right with God, but he had no access to religious rituals because he was a tax collector. Because of the proximity of Zaccheus's story to the incident described in Luke 18, some have speculated that, in fact, Zaccheus *was* the tax collector who longed to worship but who was excluded from community.

Whether that is true or not we cannot know, but we do know that Zaccheus was a tax collector, and apparently he was pretty good at it. He was not just *a* tax collector—Zaccheus was *the* tax collector for the wealthy Jericho region. This meant that he collected taxes personally, and he also took a cut from the collections harvested by other tax collectors in the area as well. He would be the organizer, supervisor, and beneficiary of all Roman revenues extorted from his Jewish brothers.

To add insult to injury, Zaccheus was marked by irony, because his name comes from the word *sacai,* which, oddly enough, means "pure." His name was an aspiration he could never attain, and because names in ancient Israel carried such great significance, you can only imagine the dreams his parents must have had for him when they gave him such a lofty name. It is less difficult to imagine the sense of heartache and grief they must have felt when seeing their son depart so clearly from Jewish life.

Pure? What a laugh! Zaccheus was filth. The scum of the earth. Yet, though he had everything the world could offer materially, this publican longed for something that would transcend his

wealth. And, again ironically, this man who seemed to have everything sought to fill his emptiness by pursuing the Jesus who said,
"one's life does not consist in the abundance of the things he possesses" (Luke 12:15 NKJV).

A Heart's Desire

Zaccheus was trying to see who Jesus was, and was unable
because of the crowd, for he was small in stature. So he
ran on ahead and climbed up into a sycamore tree in order
to see Him, for He was about to pass through that way.
(Luke 19:3–4)

When my kids were small, we lived in Holland, Michigan,
where the Dutch heritage of the community fed into an annual rite
of spring—Tulip Time. Hundreds of thousands of people would
descend on our small, Midwestern city to enjoy Dutch culture,
photograph the millions of multicolored tulips planted throughout the town, and watch parades. They were parades of kids in
Dutch costumes doing traditional Dutch folk dances and clomp-
ing from place to place in actual wooden shoes.

People came from across North America, riding on buses and
sleeping in hotels to sit on cold, steel bleachers and watch someone else's grandchildren march in parades. Meanwhile, days in
advance, the locals would stake their own claim to a patch of grass
by leaving blankets and lawn chairs to mark their spot along the
parade route.

There is something about a parade that garners people's attention—and sometimes people will go to great lengths to make sure
they have a good view. It is at this point that the story of Zaccheus,
the "wee little man" of children's Sunday school songs, feels the
most familiar to us. Yet we literally have missed the forest of ideas

presented here for the tree he was climbing. For the record, it was a sycamore fig tree that the tax collector scaled to see the parade that passed through Jericho. These trees bore several crops of figs each year and generally had slick bark, which should make it hard to climb—especially for someone vertically challenged. These sycamore fig trees, however, also had large branches near the ground level, which would help a short person to climb it more easily.

All of that is fascinating and not unimportant per se, but the reality is that the tree is primarily a prop for the larger drama that is playing out in Luke 19. The main thing is the man—not the tree. His heart's desire is to see Jesus—though we are not told why. Perhaps Zaccheus had heard that one of Christ's own followers (Matthew) had a story similar to his. Perhaps he had heard of the feast Matthew had held for Jesus, an event in which Jesus would celebrate the fact that He was a physician who had come for those most in need. Perhaps the theories are correct and Zaccheus was the tax collector of Luke 18 after all. If this is the case, he has no idea how pivotal this moment would be.

The publican in Luke 18, standing at a distance and beating his breast, cries out to God, "God, be merciful to me, the sinner!" (v. 13). Literally, he is asking for a mercy seat to receive his offerings to God, for as we have seen the temple was off-limits to him. Now coming Zaccheus's way is the Lamb of God whose blood would take away the sins of the world—an offering providing a mercy seat available to all. Including the hated tax collectors.

Whatever Zaccheus's reasons were for wanting to see Jesus, his passion is seen as he slips and slides his way up the tree to catch a view of the Teacher from Nazareth. A hated, rejected outlier, Zaccheus had endured the scorn and abuse of his countrymen for as long as he had been in his chosen profession. Now they would have fresh ammunition to aim at the chief tax collector of

Jericho. This dignified businessman exposed himself to the risk of the crowd's ridicule by scaling the tree. Let's face it, when was the last time you saw a Fortune 500 CEO climbing a tree to get a better look at the motorcade of a traveling evangelist? Exactly.

What Zaccheus was doing was ridiculous and he knew it—but that didn't matter. What mattered to him somehow and in some way was Jesus. Although Zaccheus ("the pure") may have seemed like the least pious, least religious person on that Jericho street, he may have been the one whose heart most hungered for God. As the tax collector watched the parade approach, something he had long desired was about to happen. But the way it would happen surprised him and shocked the crowd.

A Shocking Fellowship

When Jesus came to the place, He looked up and said to him, "Zaccheus, hurry and come down, for today I must stay at your house." And he hurried and came down and received Him gladly. When they saw it, they all began to grumble, saying, "He has gone to be the guest of a man who is a sinner." (Luke 19:5–7)

Many times in life, we want nothing more than to hide in plain sight—to be lost in the crowd. Many who have had struggles in their faith journey or who have been burned by bad church experiences will gravitate to a large church where they can work through their disappointments and frustrations at their own pace. They blend in, hold things at arm's length, and hope no one notices their pain—even from a distance.

If Zaccheus was hoping to find camouflage in the leaves of the sycamore fig tree, it wasn't going to work. Not only did Jesus move in his direction but the Master also stopped at Zaccheus's tree. Not only did He stop but Jesus also proceeded to look up and expose the tax collector by name. Not only did He call Zaccheus by name but Jesus, being the King that He is, also called for the publican's service to be duly rendered on His behalf. Having served the emperor of Rome, this publican is now being invited to serve a greater King.

It is fascinating that although Zaccheus apparently is seeing Jesus for the first time, the Messiah knows who the tax collector is. One even gets the strong impression that just as Jesus did with the woman at the well in John 4, He has come to Jericho specifically to encounter this wealthy yet poverty-stricken man. In the process, Jesus commandeers Zaccheus's home for what surely would have been a meal. After all, social protocols demanded that food be offered to any guest entering a home.

In the eyes of the religious leaders, it is unthinkable that a genuine prophet would soil his name by associating with a man of such tarnished reputation. Remember, Jesus selected a tax collector to be one of His inner circle of twelve disciples (Matthew/Levi). As scandalous as it was to include a tax collector as a disciple, Jesus now compounds this glaring infraction by entering Zaccheus's house and apparently dining with the people who were viewed as the most unclean and most inappropriate of the community: People who were to be despised, not engaged.

This meal bears significance, because in first-century Israel dining was not just about getting nourishment. It had many ritual overtones that affected a person's ceremonial purity. How the hands were washed, how the food was prepared, how the dishes and pots were cleaned, and, yes, who a person sat with at the table all had profound implications. These rituals affected a person's own purity to participate in temple or synagogue activities because dining with someone implied acceptance of him. And Zaccheus was unacceptable to his Jewish neighbors.

As a result, the people begin to complain and grumble at this massive "error" on Jesus's part. Zaccheus shimmies down the tree and joyfully welcomes the Savior into his home. Meanwhile, like the dark clouds of a gathering storm, the crowd—now left behind for a moment—begins to question what kind of person Jesus is after all. How could a so-called prophet be so foolish? The same crowd that moments before had been celebrating the fact that Jesus could give sight to a blind man now questions His decision to receive hospitality from a sinner of the first order.

Perhaps Bartimaeus wasn't the only blind person in Jericho. The Scriptures tell us that although man looks on the outward appearance, God looks on the heart—and Jesus's invitation to Zaccheus is evidence that this is more than just the power of observation. God looks with a different value system. The crowd is blind to the needs of this fallen, failed, corrupt human being. Jesus, however, sees him with perfect clarity and responds to the longing of Zaccheus's heart for access to the God he had abandoned in his pursuit of wealth.

Jesus's willingness to be the "friend of sinners" was so tangible, so bold that we must see in it the heart of the Father. To think that the holy God who created and rules the universe would make room for any of us in His house and family speaks loudly to how He views us. We are all fallen, broken image-bearers who are nevertheless the objects of His great, overwhelming, rescuing love. Not because we are healthy but because we are so desperately needy of Him. Just like Zaccheus.

The one standing afar off is drawn near. The one who had climbed a tree now reclines at the table. The one who had been lost is now found—and He offers substantial evidence of the profound change his time with Jesus has made on his heart.

A Changed Heart

Zaccheus stopped and said to the Lord, "Behold, Lord, half of my possessions I will give to the poor, and if I have defrauded anyone of anything, I will give back four times as much." And Jesus said to him, "Today salvation has come to this house, because he, too, is a son of Abraham." (Luke 19:8–9)

It has been said that nothing will have an impact on us more during the course of any year than the books we read and the people we meet. I'm pretty sure that in the very least Zaccheus would agree with the second half of that claim. He has just met Jesus, and the impact of that meeting will become clear to everyone in the Jericho region where Zaccheus, the chief tax collector, has plied his trade.

It is important to note that there is apparently a time lapse that occurs between verses 7 and 8. The crowd is still waiting outside and no doubt still complaining. Jesus is dining with publicans and sinners. How long does this encounter go on? What was the tenor of the conversation? We are not told. What we *are* told, however, is the meeting's outcome.

As they exit his home, Zaccheus announces, first to Jesus and then to the gathered crowd, "Behold, Lord, half of my possessions I will give to the poor, and if I have defrauded anyone of anything, I will give back four times as much." This declaration has two parts, and both are extremely important.

In Judaism, one of the greatest indications of piety was concern for the poor—and Zaccheus is breaking the bank to make up for lost time in this area. Committing to give up half of all he owns in order to serve the needs of "the least" of his Jewish brothers makes a bold statement that this is a radically different man than the one who had climbed the tree. Keep in mind as well that, no doubt, many of the poor he is offering to help are in that condition because of Zaccheus's own past extortionate tax-collecting methods. The new value system that motivates Zaccheus's generosity stands in bold contrast to the rich young ruler who, when challenged by Jesus about his wealth and the needs of the poor, went away sorrowful (Luke 18:23) because of his possessions. Zaccheus doesn't even flinch—he offers half of his goods to that selfsame cause.

Then the tax collector goes even further. He is willing to give compensation for any he had defrauded (v. 8). This is a dramatic offer, because in all likelihood Zaccheus had defrauded *everyone*. That was what publicans did. What little wealth he may have had remaining after responding to the needs of the poor would clearly be exhausted in fulfilling this dramatic promise.

Zaccheus's commitment is an act of grace. Moses's law (Exodus 22:1–4) called for restitution to be made when someone has been robbed, but the guilty party was only expected to double the amount stolen. Only in a case where the theft was part of a deliberate and violent act was it to be repaid fourfold. While tax collecting in ancient Israel was deliberate, it was seldom violent in nature. Who needed violence when the might of Rome stood at your side?

As such, Zaccheus's words are external indications of an internal change of heart. The greed that had driven Zaccheus his entire adult life was now seen to be of no significance. The wealth and money that had seemed so important before now has no hold on Zaccheus's life. His changed values were the evidence of a changed spirit. I don't know about you, but that makes me even more curious about what Jesus might have said to Zaccheus as they dined together.

Although we don't know what Jesus said to him behind closed

doors, we do know what the Master said to the crowd outside in the harsh light of day, "Today salvation has come to this house, because he, too, is a son of Abraham" (Luke 19:9). The rescue of the publican's heart has been evidenced by the transformation of his attitude toward life, people, wealth, and God.

It seems to me that when Jesus declared Zaccheus to be a son of Abraham, that new identity had nothing to do with ethnicity. It had everything to do with a heart that was now willing to walk by faith, not by sight. Paul would later explain this transaction for all believers: "Even so Abraham BELIEVED GOD, AND IT WAS RECKONED TO HIM AS RIGHTEOUSNESS. Therefore, be sure that it is those who are of faith who are sons of Abraham" (Galatians 3:6–7).

Zaccheus was a son of Abraham because his heart had been drawn to God in faith, and as with his ancient forbear that trust in God shaped how he approached life in the present tense.

A Call to Mercy

"For the Son of Man has come to seek and to save that which was lost." (Luke 19:10)

Jesus's final words to Zaccheus once again state and reflect His mission—a mission of rescue, redemption, and restoration. What Jesus did in a lunch meeting with the chief tax collector of Jericho was, like so much of what the Savior did, an anticipation of the cross.

From that cross would come a call to all who are lost. A call from the One who came to seek and save. A call to relationship and return. A call to new life in Christ, made abundant by His presence and power. A call to experience mercy and grace rather than condemnation and law. A call to everyone—from the worst sinner to the most self-righteous religionist.

Jesus was always on-mission. But the encounter with Zaccheus is a reminder of just how merciful God's mercy is and just how gracious God's grace is. It reaches to all—even short people—with hope and light and peace. As the old hymn affirms:

> Depth of mercy! Can there be
> Mercy still reserved for me?
> Can my God His wrath forbear,
> Me, the chief of sinners, spare?
> I have long withstood His grace,
> Long provoked Him to His face,
> Would not hearken to His calls,
> Grieved Him by a thousand falls.
> Kindled His relentings are:
> Me He now delights to spare;
> Cries, "How shall I give Thee up?"
> Lets the lifted thunder drop.
> There for me the Savior stands,
> Holding forth His wounded hands;
> God is love! I know, I feel;
> Jesus weeps and loves me still.
> —*Charles Wesley, 1740*

A Heart That Forgives
Jesus and a Guilty Woman

I am firmly convinced that if Word War II had not happened, the History Channel would not exist. It seems that the vast majority of this network's programming either deals with the war in general or Hitler in particular. Hitler's bodyguards. Hitler's hideouts. Hitler and the occult. The list goes on and on—and people watch. There is something spellbinding about unnatural, unmitigated evil that draws us in.

Such was the case with one of those series, *Hitler's Henchmen*, which featured Dr. Josef Mengele. I was interested in this one because in high school I read a biography of Mengele, which described the horrific work of the man dubbed "The Angel of Death." Mengele used the Jewish prisoners as if they were laboratory animals, performing unspeakable experiments of the most bizarre nature, unconcerned about the implications of the Hippocratic Oath he had once sworn and uncaring about the excruciating agony he was inflicting on his fellow human beings.

Perhaps *that* was the problem. To Mengele, the Jewish prisoners of Auschwitz were not human. They were objects to be used to quench his thirsty curiosity. Objects to be used, not people to be loved.

Years later, pop singer B. J. Thomas recorded a song that while simple in melody carried a weighty reminder. It was titled "Using

Things and Loving People." The point? When we get that turned around and begin loving things and using people, life tends to go off the rails. Things are not to get in the way of loving others. We have a spiritual duty, calling, and privilege to love people. When questioned about the intent of Moses's law, Jesus presented what is often called the "great command" saying:

> "The foremost is, 'HEAR, O ISRAEL! THE LORD OUR GOD IS ONE LORD; AND YOU SHALL LOVE THE LORD YOUR GOD WITH ALL YOUR HEART, AND WITH ALL YOUR SOUL, AND WITH ALL YOUR MIND, AND WITH ALL YOUR STRENGTH.' The second is this, 'YOU SHALL LOVE YOUR NEIGHBOR AS YOURSELF.' There is no other commandment greater than these." (Mark 12:29–31)

Later, Paul affirmed this by adding: "For the whole Law is fulfilled in one word, in the statement, 'YOU SHALL LOVE YOUR NEIGHBOR AS YOURSELF'" (Galatians 5:14).

The message is clear: people are to be loved, not used. Yet even in Jesus's day, using people to accomplish selfish aims—even at the risk of that individual's great personal harm—was not beyond those who should have been most committed to the great command. In John 8 we see what happens when the Jewish religious leaders are willing to see a woman killed in order to entrap Jesus. Using people.

The Trap Is Set

Early in the morning [Jesus] came again into the temple, and all the people were coming to Him; and He sat down and began to teach them. The scribes and the Pharisees brought a woman caught in adultery, and having set her in the center of the court, they said to Him, "Teacher, this woman has been caught in adultery, in the very act. Now in the Law Moses commanded us to stone such women; what then do You say?" They were saying this, testing Him, so that they might have grounds for accusing Him. (John 8:2–6)

Our criminal justice system has standards detailing how law enforcement authorities may and may not go about their work. One of these regulations is that the suspect is protected against tactics of entrapment. In entrapment scenarios, the police construct a situation that might induce a suspect into committing a crime he otherwise may not have committed.

Entrapment is not merely bad form. It is considered a blow to the integrity of the justice system, and it can be cited as a defense in criminal court cases. John 8:6 makes it clear that the intent behind this event is to create a scenario in which Jesus will misspeak and entrap himself with His own words, and the religious leaders are willing to use a woman as bait on the hook to lure Jesus into self-entrapment—even if she might be killed in the process. Again, using people.

Before we look at this critical event, it is important to recognize that some translations of the Bible will bracket this entire section and footnote it with a statement that this passage is not found in the oldest manuscripts. As such, many scholars view it as suspect. I will be the first to confess that I am not an expert in textual criticism. I have read the arguments for and against certain manuscript families, and I have seen the resulting approaches to how the text of the Bible is presented.

Since I am not an expert in such matters, however, I use a simple (admittedly subjective) test to determine how I will approach a biblical text—the "eye test." I look at the event in question, and in this case what Jesus is doing and how He is conducting himself. Then I ask myself, "Does this event seem to be consistent with the heart and attitude of Jesus as He is portrayed throughout the Gospels?"

Here the answer is a resounding "Yes." This is precisely how we would expect Jesus to deal with a woman like this. He is often portrayed as dining with "tax collectors and sinners." In fact, we have already seen that Jesus happily accepts the label "the friend of sinners" (Luke 7:34). His dealings with this woman harmonize with this title with beautiful consistency. From my perspective, I will step back from the textual debate and let the story stand because it clearly represents what we have come to know and love about the heart of our Savior. Let's think through it together.

The Religionists' Charge

Notice that it is early in the morning as Jesus has come into the temple to teach. As the crowd is listening, there is a rising tide of noise and confusion coming from the back of the group. Slowly the crowd parts and a woman, being dragged forward by the officially robed scribes and Pharisees, is thrust before Jesus. There is amazing contrast here, as we see the official and officious look of these religious leaders contrasted to this woman. It is likely, given their description of her, that her clothes are askew and that she looks a bit of a mess. Why? Because she has just been caught committing the act of adultery.

Dragged from her bed, she becomes the object with which they desire to entrap Jesus. The charge against her? "Teacher, this woman has been caught in adultery, in the very act. Now in the Law Moses commanded us to stone such women; what then do You say?" (John 8:4–5).

Clearly, this is a serious charge because, as the religionists point out, Moses's law states that this woman has committed a capital offense. And it is important to notice that neither the woman nor Jesus in any way refutes the charge against her. She is guilty; therefore, she is deserving of the penalty prescribed in Moses's law—death by stoning.

The point of all this is to impale Jesus on the proverbial horns of a dilemma. A dilemma is when you have two options and no matter which one you select, you are in trouble. Here is the dilemma facing Jesus:

> ***Option 1:*** Show mercy and compassion to this guilty woman and demand that she be set free. The dilemma? If Jesus refuses to have her stoned, He will be seen as defying the law of Moses and His teaching and ministry will be discredited.

> ***Option 2:*** Order her execution by stoning, thereby affirming Jesus's allegiance to Moses. The dilemma? In the Roman Empire, only the Roman government (John 18:31) was allowed to execute capital punishment. If Jesus orders the woman's death, he is in violation of Roman law and can be handed over to Roman authorities for His own execution.

Either way, Jesus is in trouble—either with the people of Israel or with the government of Rome.

The Real Truth

Nothing about this event is a coincidence—it must be understood that this was a staged event. Remember, the purpose of this setup is to test Jesus in order to discredit Him.

In John 7:45–52, we find that the night before this event the religious leaders had met in a secret conclave. They had ordered the temple police to arrest Jesus and bring Him to them, but those guards were so taken by Jesus's teaching that they couldn't bring themselves to arrest Him! The frustration of the religious establishment is clear as they try to come to a consensus with which to judge Jesus—even though they could not get everyone on the same page. It seems apparent that this staged event is their attempt to provide ironclad proof that Jesus is a danger to the people, to the law, and to themselves—and must be removed.

But these champions of Moses's law are also subtly manipulating that law in order to entrap Jesus. Moses wrote:

> If a man is found lying with a married woman, then both of them shall die, the man who lay with the woman, and the woman; thus you shall purge the evil from Israel. . . . then you shall bring them both out to the gate of that city and you shall stone them to death; the girl, because she did not cry out in the city, and the man, because he has violated his neighbor's wife. (Deuteronomy 22:22, 24)

The obvious question is this: "Where is the man?" Certainly, this woman was not committing adultery by herself, yet the man she was sleeping with is nowhere to be found. Why? Because it was a setup. Apparently, the religious leaders were not only willing to let this woman be stoned to death in order to entrap Jesus but they were also willing to allow some unidentified, unarrested Jewish man to commit the sin of adultery so they would have a guilty woman to use as bait in the trap they were setting for Jesus.

All of this is staged in order to destroy Jesus—but they are quite happy to have the sin of adultery committed and a woman killed if that is what it would take to accomplish their goals. Loving things. In this case, power. Using people. In this case, the accused woman and the missing man.

How would Jesus react to this blatant attempt to manipulate justice?

The Savior's Reaction

"But Jesus stooped down and with His finger wrote on the ground." (John 8:6)

Imagine the scene as they all hold their breath, waiting for Jesus to respond. Instead of speaking to the woman or her accusers, though, He stoops down and writes in the dirt at His feet.

This is amazing. There are three times in the Bible when we see God actually writing:

- The writing of the Ten Commandments on stone. "When He had finished speaking with him upon Mount Sinai, He gave Moses the two tablets of the testimony, tablets of stone, written by the finger of God" (Exodus 31:18).
- The writing of judgment upon a wall (Daniel 5:5, "Suddenly the fingers of a man's hand emerged and began writing opposite the lampstand on the plaster of the wall of the king's palace, and the king saw the back of the hand that did the writing.")
- The writing of mercy in the dust (here)

One of the great questions scholars have wrestled with over the years has been this: What did Jesus write? The answers range from the humorous (Jesus wrote the names of women that these religious leaders had inappropriately been with), to the honest (we don't know because the text doesn't tell us), to the heavy (Jesus was writing a condemnation of the sin of the people in general). Yet, Bible teacher J. Vernon McGee (1904–1988) suggested a possibility that lines up perfectly with one of the themes of John's gospel record—the theme of living waters.

Notice the words of the Old Testament prophet Jeremiah: "O LORD, the hope of Israel, all who forsake You shall be ashamed. 'Those who depart from Me Shall be *written in the earth,* because they have forsaken the LORD, the fountain of living waters'" (Jeremiah 17:13, NKJV; emphasis mine).

In John 7, as Jesus taught in the temple, He had reasserted something He had previously declared in John 4. Notice these two statements:

- Jesus answered and said to her, "Everyone who drinks of this water will thirst again; but whoever drinks of the water that I will give him shall never thirst; but the water that I will give him will become in him a well of water springing up to eternal life" (John 4:13–14).
- Now on the last day, the great day of the feast, Jesus stood and cried out, saying, "If anyone is thirsty, let him come to Me and drink. He who believes in Me, as the Scripture said, 'From his innermost being will flow rivers of living water'" (John 7:37–38).

One of the strategies John uses in presenting his telling of the story of Jesus is, as John Stott said, the strategy of *fulfillment.* In John's gospel, Jesus makes remarkable claims for both His identity and His mission, and then He does things to back up those claims. He claims to be the bread of life, then (John 6) feeds a hungry multitude from a kid's sack lunch. He claims to be the light of the world, then proves it by giving sight (John 9; see chapter 11) to a man who had been born blind.

Here, Jesus is repeating His claim to be living water by bringing true and meaningful life to a woman who is clearly broken by her life and her choices—though that living water is being rejected by the religionists attempting to orchestrate her death.

So, then, after writing in the dirt, what does Jesus do?

The Savior's Response

But when they persisted in asking Him, He straightened up, and said to them, "He who is without sin among you, let him be the first to throw a stone at her." Again He stooped down and wrote on the ground. When they heard it, they began to go out one by one, beginning with the older ones, and He was left alone, and the woman, where she was, in the center of the court. (John 8:7–9)

When the Israelites were leaving Egypt under Moses's leadership, they found themselves trapped between the Red Sea and the armies of Pharaoh. If they were to go forward, they would have had the problem of the uncrossable sea. If they were to go backwards, they would have the problem of the Egyptian cavalry. This is the essence of a dilemma—and a parallel to the dilemma that Jesus is facing in John 8. His response, however, is to take himself out of the crosshairs of this attempt at entrapment and place those crosshairs firmly on the religious leaders who are so sadly out of the step with the God they claim to represent.

In the military, one of the phrases that has become emblematic of the modern approach to warfare is "rules of engagement." The point of such rules is to inform soldiers what is and what is not viewed as an acceptable approach to engaging the opposition. To this point in John 8, these religious leaders think they have been firmly in control of the rules of engagement as they take on their great enemy—Jesus. And those rules of engagement seem to have very few limitations. But before they even know what has happened, Jesus takes control of the situation and changes the rules of engagement.

Suddenly, the issue is not about Jesus's credibility or the woman's guilt. Jesus turns the table by making the issue about who is (and who is not) qualified to judge another human being. As you visualize this situation playing out, you envision the mingling together of the crowd that had gathered to hear Jesus and the mob that had brought the woman. How do you tell which group is which? Undoubtedly, the lynch mob has come prepared with stones to use in executing this woman—even though they would most likely prefer to stone Jesus instead of the woman.

Jesus forces their hand with His cryptic challenge, "He who is without sin among you, let him be the first to throw a stone at her" (John 8:7). The issue is not the woman's guilt or innocence—it is the men's own guilt or innocence! To apply the standard they are demanding, Jesus does not set the standard as "one who has not committed the sin of adultery." The standard necessary in order for someone to be qualified to pronounce judgment on another person is absolute. You must be "without sin." Which, by the way, is why God alone is qualified to judge sin in human beings.

The charade of religious righteousness has been exposed. Because they know they cannot claim utter sinlessness, these men—so happy to use, destroy, entrap, and judge others—slink away in embarrassment. Beginning with the oldest, the ones driven more by cool reason than the heat of emotion, they drop the stones with a dramatic thud and escape to plot other ways to attempt to destroy Jesus.

The Rescue Completed

Straightening up, Jesus said to her, "Woman, where are they? Did no one condemn you?" She said, "No one, Lord." And Jesus said, "I do not condemn you, either. Go. From now on sin no more." (John 8:10–11)

Have you ever been caught with your hand in the proverbial cookie jar? It can be embarrassing and even humiliating, but most of all it can be threatening, because our guilt is out in the open and can't be hidden with fig leaves of our own design (see Genesis 3).

Put yourself in this woman's place. She knows she is guilty, and she also knows that she is being used. In a sense she was used sexually by the man she had slept with, and now she is being used by men who are supposed to be spiritual leaders. This manipulation, however, is intensified by the fact that it is being done out in the open, in the sight of the public. She has no place to hide and nowhere to run. How must she have felt as this scene has unfolded?

She is both of two things:

Publicly charged: This incident was a trap specifically prepared to catch Jesus. The religious leaders rudely forced their way into the center of the group and interrupted Jesus's teaching. As Jesus is seated in the temple area, here come these men dragging a woman whose clothes are in disarray and whose hair is disheveled—defiant and resisting them. The lesson is interrupted as the crowd turns to see what all the fuss is about—and the religious leaders fling her into the midst of the group where Jesus is teaching and make their crude charge: "We caught her in the act of adultery!"

Genuinely guilty: The guilt of the woman was indisputable; she had been "caught in the act." There is no indication here that Jesus challenged the charge; in fact, He did refer to it as sin.

The point? She was guilty—there was no doubt of that. But in a sense, that is not the point here. The point is this: how will Jesus respond to her, and will it be any different from the way these other men have—as an object to be used?

Finally, for the first time, Jesus addresses the woman personally. Still a dilemma remains.

What about condemnation? Jesus straightened up and addressed the woman, "Woman, where are they? Did no one condemn you?" His address was respectful. Her accusers had made her the bait for a trap. They were more interested in destroying Jesus than in saving her. But their vicious hatred of Him was as bad as her immorality. Jesus's rebuke had prevented their executing her, and her response is one of respect and submission, "No one, Lord!" It is the heart that views Him as different from her hypocritical accusers—and she seems ready to accept whatever judgment He chooses to apply.

What about compassion? Of all the people there, only Jesus is qualified to pronounce sentence upon her! He is without sin altogether and can condemn, if He chooses. But Jesus did not pronounce a sentence on her either. At the same time, in the midst of this display of mercy, neither did He proclaim her to be innocent. He does not excuse her sin or pretend it didn't happen. He judges it while exercising a grace that could save her.

What about correction? Jesus's words are strong, "Go. From now on sin no more" (John 8:11). Meeting a man who was more interested in saving than exploiting and in forgiving rather than condemning must have been a new experience for her. Jesus's attitude provided both the motivation and the warning she needed. Forgiveness demands a clean break with sin. She must live the changed life forgiveness produces—and abandon this life of sin. This is not a small thing, but it is a corrective that Jesus applies in love, rather than wielding it as a weapon.

For perhaps the first time in a long time, someone views her as a person and not a thing. For the first time, someone interacts with her with a real concern for her well-being and not for his selfish ends. For the first time in a long time, she feels warmth of compassion—albeit with strict words of correction and discipline—and remembers what it feels like to be a human being. Jesus responds to her with grace.

Jesus's interaction with this woman—who was apparently accustomed to being used but not accustomed to being loved—is a powerful reminder that our lives are both past and present. The product of our past needs to be resolved in the present in order to secure our future. And the key behind that resolution is the grace of our Lord. He deals directly with her problems, but then He encourages her to a future that is pointed toward life and away from the self-destructive bent of her past. Grace is the heart of God that loves people. And nowhere is that grace more clearly seen than in the life of one who fully and completely knows her own personal undeservedness.

❖ ❖ ❖

How do you weigh the worth of a human being? In the military, combat means lives are exchanged for land. Those lives are defined in terms of "acceptable losses." For example, on D-Day during World War II—June 6, 1944— historians estimate that there were some 10,000 Allied casualties on the Normandy beaches. Those tragic losses were considered "acceptable" by Allied commanders. The lives themselves have value in that they advanced the cause of the battle to stop the Axis powers.

But such thinking is not limited to theatres of war. Utilitarian views of things and people mark our culture to the point where human worth is scuttled under an avalanche of manipulation. How vital it is in such a world to live with the heart of Jesus, one that reflects the heart of the Father. This heart loves and never uses—even to the point of expressing love in absolute self-sacrifice. As Jesus said, "Greater love has no one than this, that one lay down his life for his friends" (John 15:13).

His friends were seen by the religionists as sinners who were unwanted, unwelcome, and unworthy. Jesus extends love and grace to His friends who in fact should have been His enemies. This, the practical embodiment and extension of the mind of Christ in His followers, was the thought that drove the hymn writer to pen:

> May the mind of Christ, my Savior,
> Live in me from day to day,
> By His love and power controlling
> All I do and say.
> May the peace of God, my Father,
> Rule my life in everything,
> That I may be calm to comfort
> Sick and sorrowing.
> May the love of Jesus fill me,
> As the waters fill the sea;

Him exalting, self abasing–
This is victory.

>   —*Kate B. Wilkinson, 1925*

ELEVEN

A Heart That Values

Jesus and a Man Born Blind

John Godfrey Saxe's story from the Indian subcontinent has become one of the world's most enduring parables on perspective. It tells of six blind men who hear that an elephant is in town, so they go to "see" what an elephant is like. Using their sense of touch, each blind man locates a part of the elephant and feels it. Later, when questioned as to the nature of an elephant, each blind man had a different answer. The one who had touched a leg said an elephant is like a tree. The blind man who had felt the trunk described an elephant as a snake. The one who grabbed the tail said that an elephant resembled a rope.

The point? Each of them was initially right but all of them were ultimately wrong. Their perspective was limited to the information available to them—but that information was incomplete. As a result, their answers were likewise incomplete, though not completely incorrect. They had rooted their descriptions in their perspectives, and those perspectives were flawed.

Much of the time, life is fully and completely about perspective. Whether we see an event as comedy or tragedy comes down to perspective. Whether we see a moment as threat or opportunity is a matter of perspective. And how we view people also has a way of betraying our perspective—and the heart that gives birth to that perspective.

The story of the blind men and the elephant is particularly appropriate here, because in John 9 Jesus encounters a man who had been born blind. And the variety of the perspectives coming from the people who encounter this man are instructive about how differently various people view others.

As John introduces the story, some perspective (pardon the continuing emphasis) is important. In John 8, we see Jesus dealing with the "sinful" woman and declaring himself to be the Light of the world (John 8:12). This declaration leads to yet another—and one of the most intense—debates between Jesus and the religious leaders found anywhere in the Gospels. As the two sides wage verbal combat, Jesus ultimately declares His identity as completely entwined with the Father by stating quite unambiguously, "Truly, truly, I say to you, before Abraham was born, I am" (John 8:58).

Claiming that He had predated the ancient and revered father of the Jewish people was, apparently, the last straw for some in this ongoing religious battle. These religionists are so incensed by Jesus's claim (making himself eternal, and, as such, equal to the God of Abraham) that they spontaneously form a first-century lynch mob and prepare to stone Jesus to death, which they had wanted to do when they brought the "sinful" woman to Him (John 8).

While the religious leaders' actions are fairly straightforward, Jesus's actions are less clear. John says, "Jesus hid Himself and went out of the temple" (John 8:59). How did He hide from these people He had just been debating? Where could He go to escape from their ever-present and intensifying threat? John doesn't tell us. He only says that Jesus and His followers left the temple.

The King James Version, however, presents the moment with a twist that is intentionally designed to set up the next event in Jesus's public ministry. That translation reads, "Jesus hid himself, and went out of the temple, going through the midst of them, and so passed by."

"And so passed by." That small statement will become increasingly important as we move deeper into our consideration of the story.

Riddle Me This—The Disciples' View

In the Batman comic books, one of Batman's criminal foes was a character known as "The Riddler." The Riddler's trademark was that he challenged the Caped Crusader with the words, "Riddle me this . . ." Clues in the cases and crimes that involved The Riddler were always presented in the form of riddles that had to be unpacked in order to solve the crime. It was an eccentric game of cat and mouse that became the modus operandi of one of Batman's most persistent opponents.

This idea of riddles and their answers is not limited to caped superheroes and their archenemies. In theological circles, debate is sometimes rooted in the fact that the Scriptures often present events or ideas in mysteries, symbols, metaphors, or, yes, riddles. As theological scholars freshly trained at the feet of Jesus, the disciples gravitate toward the concept of riddle as they ponder the circumstances of this man who had been born blind—and that predisposition fills in the blanks of their collective perspective of this man and his condition: "As He passed by, He saw a man blind from birth. And His disciples asked Him, 'Rabbi, who sinned, this man or his parents, that he would be born blind?'" (John 9:1–2).

Blindness was rampant in the first century because of the prevailing unsanitary conditions. In a culture where work almost exclusively depended upon a person's ability to see, there were no career options for a blind man. The sightless person's only career path was to become a beggar and live off the kindness and generosity of strangers who, because they were sighted, were able to work.

Apparently the blind man in this passage was a fixture at the temple, hoping that people coming to and from worship would give some money. It would have been quite normal to see a variety of beggars at the various temple gates, since the Mosaic law had much to say about caring for and providing for the poor—and this beggar was among the poorest of the poor.

This blind man is the very picture of destitute poverty. He would be disheveled, unkempt, ragged, and humiliated. And this fed into people's perceptions of him. In first-century Israel, people believed in what operated as the "Law of Retribution," which asserted that the righteous were blessed according to their righteousness and the wicked were cursed according to their wickedness. It was their way of seeking to explain tragedies in life. From a New Testament angle, we might call it the "law of sowing and reaping." In other words, all of life's difficulties were judgment for sin.

The conclusion? This man's blindness was a consequence of sin. So the only question that remains is whose sin is to blame? As the disciples view this man, it is this theological riddle they want to work through with Jesus. This man's hurt, humiliation, and anguish seem to be totally lost on Jesus's disciples. They only see him as an interesting riddle to solve.

The theological conundrum is seen in the question, "Who sinned?" If the parents sinned, the facts before the disciples become pretty straightforward. Sometimes, congenital blindness is a result of sexually transmitted diseases (which implies the presence of sinful sexual activity) that can affect the child as he or she travels through the birth canal. That part is pretty easy to sort out.

But if the man himself is the guilty party, how do you explain that? To our way of thinking, it seems to be an absurd statement.

How could a person commit sin before he is even born? Shockingly, in the religious thinking of some rabbis in Israel at the time, there were three possible answers to the riddle:

- **Predestinarian view.** In this view, the suffering individual was being judged in advance for the sinful choices he would make later in life.
- **Prenatal view.** Here the idea is that the man actually could have sinned in the womb, and it was such a heinous sin that he was cursed with congenital blindness.
- **Past-life view.** Some ancient rabbis actually taught a form of reincarnation, where the suffering of this life is attributed to sins committed in a past life.

In Israel's theological paradigm, the question "Who sinned?" was not only legitimate but it is also seen by many as the only question that really mattered. However, they were actually asking the wrong question. The rest of the New Testament tells us that suffering in this life can actually be for a variety of reasons:

- Sometimes suffering may be the product of divine correction.
- Sometimes suffering is God's instrument in developing our faith or our character.
- Sometimes suffering is merely the byproduct of living in a broken world.
- Sometimes suffering is to equip us to help others when they suffer.

Nevertheless, how often do we react as did the disciples? Tragedy may have a victim, but we often lean toward the idea that it also demands a culprit. And if it happened to *them* (whoever that is), they probably deserved it. Our presuppositions and perspectives are not that different from the disciples of Jesus in the first century.

In this scenario, however, something significant was taking place. The man is blind but he is not deaf. He may not be able to see those speaking, but he hears this intellectual exercise going on in front of him as if he wasn't even there. The impression given is that to the disciples this real man and his real pain are irrelevant. Of first importance to them was the need to sort out a theological riddle.

The Power of Mystery—The Neighbors' View

In England stands Stonehenge, the giant rock formations that have seemingly stood there forever. How did they get there? Who put them in place? In Egypt, the ancient pyramids rise above the desert as giant burial grounds that are one of the seven wonders of the ancient world. But who built them, and how? Even with the massive human resource of the Hebrew slave force, what was the methodology used to construct those massive edifices? In Peru are the Nazca lines—giant ground carvings that form all kinds of perfectly symmetrical shapes or clearly distinct creatures. But those shapes can only be seen from high above ground level—from the air. How did those lines get there, and for what purpose?

All three of these examples have one thing in common—mystery. For generations, scholars and scientists have tried to unravel the mysteries of how these things could have been built by ancient civilizations without the technological or industrial means seemingly necessary to accomplish them. For some, it is this sense of mystery that gives these amazing sites their allure and interest. For others, they can't leave it alone. Such a situation requires intense study to try and solve the mystery.

The same is true in the mystery of the supernatural. People look at the stories of the Bible and try to determine scientific or rational explanations for that which can only be explained by a force outside of nature itself. A force that is *supernatural*. Once Jesus has healed the man-born-blind (we'll look at that part of the story a bit later), the neighbors who had known him all of his life were suddenly confronted with a profound mystery.

> Therefore the neighbors, and those who previously saw him as a beggar, were saying, "Is not this the one who used to sit and beg?" Others were saying, "This is he," still others were saying, "No, but he is like him." He kept saying, "I am the one." So they were saying to him, "How then were your eyes opened?" He answered, "The man who is called Jesus made clay, and anointed my eyes, and said to me, 'Go to Siloam and wash'; so I went away and washed, and I received sight." They said to him, "Where is He?" He said, "I do not know." (John 9:8–12)

Talk about mysteries! As the neighbors talk (which, by the way, seems to be universally true of neighbors everywhere), they just don't know what to make of him. Some question whether it is even the same man, but he undeniably identifies himself as that formerly blind beggar.

Immediately they want to know *how* he gained his sight, and when hearing that a Man named Jesus was at the heart of it, they want to see Him. Their apparent skepticism is part of human nature, as if we are all secretly from Missouri, the "Show Me State," where people don't believe something if they didn't see it happen.

The formerly blind man offers his personal account of his encounter with Jesus. In fact, he outlines the interaction in clear and specific detail. Notice that the man refers to the mud that

Jesus applied to his eyes as an anointing, seemingly attributing spiritual and ritual connotations to it. Jesus made mud and put it on the man's sightless eyes, then He ordered him to wash them out.

The resulting evidence of transformation is a mystery of performance but clearly not a mystery of result. This man can now see. What does that say about the One who opened his eyes? To the neighbors, all such questions are shrouded in mystery.

Doubt as Default—The Religionists' View

In the gospel records, we continually see Jesus in conflict with the religious leaders, and often the conflict is rooted in a common cause—Jesus has once again violated Sabbath law by healing a broken human being. This created no small amount of angst for the establishment, and that angst had to be resolved in terms that would neatly fit into their religious package. In fact, I think Jesus restored the man's sight by this method as a way to expose just how badly out of step the religionists' hearts were with the heart of their God.

In their nearly rabid attempts to protect the law and the Sabbath, the Pharisees were ignoring two enormous realities—the power of Christ to heal at all, Sabbath or not, and the needs of people who were intruding on their theological box.

As we return to the man who had been born blind, we see the religious leaders and their view of this man—for they view him not as a rescued heart to celebrate but as a problem to be solved.

They brought to the Pharisees the man who was formerly blind. Now it was a Sabbath on the day when Jesus made the clay and opened his eyes. They reviled him and said, "You are His disciple, but we are disciples of Moses. We know that God has spoken to Moses, but as for this man, we do not know where He is from." The man answered and said to them, "Well, here is an amazing thing, that you do not know where He is from, and yet He opened my eyes. We know that God does not hear sinners; but if anyone is God-fearing and does His will, He hears him. Since the beginning of time it has never been heard that anyone opened the eyes of a person born blind. If this man were not from God, He could do nothing." They answered him, "You were born entirely in sins, and are you teaching us?" So they put him out. (John 9:13–14, 28–34)

Of critical importance here is the phrase, "it was a Sabbath on the day when Jesus made the clay" (v. 14). By making clay, Jesus had, in their minds, violated the Sabbath prohibitions regarding work. Since they cannot explain the miracle Jesus has performed, the Pharisees respond by trying to discredit Him. And when the ex-blind man defends the character of a Man who could perform such a deed, they attack the blind man.

Notice the rising level of the conflict and the intensifying manner of the debate. The formerly blind man makes a brilliant point in this debate, "Since the beginning of time it has never been heard that anyone opened the eyes of a person born blind. If this man were not from God, He could do nothing." To him, it is as easy as connecting the dots. It is as simple as heavenly math.

> No mere man has ever been able to do this
> + Jesus is able to do this
> Jesus is no mere man. He must be from God.

Here we see the religionists in all of their legalistic determination to uphold the rules—even at the expense of people who are hurting. To these religious leaders, this man's condition and healing seem to be unimportant. In the very least, his well-being is not as important as keeping the rules. All that matters is that the law has been broken—and someone must pay for that violation.

As a result, anyone who would so blatantly violate the Sabbath regulations was automatically suspect, even if that person is able to do the impossible and even if He has just healed an adult of congenital blindness. All that matters to the religionists is protecting the Sabbath rituals.

What they failed to factor in, however, is the arrival of the Lord of the Sabbath (Matthew 12:8, Mark 2:28, Luke 6:5). The fact that Jesus can do the impossible should recalibrate their thinking about what is possible, and this should force them to rethink what the Sabbath is really about. Driven by their doubts, they miss the point of the miracle and the identity of the miracle worker.

The Power of Fear—The Parents' View

Art Linkletter made a career of putting children on display. He would gather a bunch of youngsters in front of a camera, ask them questions, and wait to see what happened next. Linkletter's strategy made for wildly unpredictable television.

But not all such displays are comfortable or charming—especially for the parents. I'm sure there were more than a few times when kids would respond in extreme ways that the mom and dad found cringeworthy. One person's entertainment becomes another's humiliation. Parenting can be pretty tough because throughout the course of life moms and dads find their greatest joys and their deepest pains wrapped up in their children.

This is the next reality we see in the experience of this blind man. Having failed to discredit Jesus or unravel the claims of the man who was healed, the Pharisees turn their substantial resources toward the purpose of breaking down the man's parents.

> The Jews then did not believe it of him, that he had been blind and had received sight, until they called the parents of the very one who had received his sight, and questioned them, saying, "Is this your son, who you say was born blind? Then how does he now see?" His parents answered them and said, "We know that this is our son, and that he was born blind; but how he now sees, we do not know; or who opened his eyes, we do not know. Ask him; he is of age, he will speak for himself." His parents said this because they were afraid of the Jews; for the Jews had already agreed that if anyone confessed Him to be Christ, he was to be put out of the synagogue. For this reason his parents said, "He is of age; ask him." (John 9:18–23)

The parents are frightened. The fact of the threat is real and the scope of the threat is overwhelming. As we have seen already, community was everything and participating in the temple/synagogue life was the core of the community's existence. To be put out of the synagogue was to be blackballed. Shunned. Excommunicated. Declared to be "as if dead." These parents were put into the impossible situation of having to reject their son so they themselves wouldn't be rejected by the most important aspect of Jewish life—participation in community. Brutal.

This is the fear of being ostracized—of being put out of the camp or the club or the group. Even with their own son, the fear inflicted by the social pressure of the religious leaders seems to overwhelm them in what should otherwise be the only normal parental response to such a miracle—celebration.

In some ways, the man's parents are the most sympathetic figures in this story. I can imagine that when their little boy was born they were devastated to discover his blindness. They must have prayed a thousand times for a miracle—for some kind of divine intervention that would rescue their son and make him whole. How desperately they must have longed for the very thing that has just happened!

Yet instead of being able to rejoice and celebrate their son's rescue from a life of blindness, they are forced to dodge the questions of the religious leaders. Their joy is muted by the terror of being cast aside. The pressure to force people into acquiescence is a diabolical weapon in the hands of the powerful to subdue the weak. And the blind man's parents lose the joy of celebration because of the oppressive power play of the religious leaders.

A Personal Love—Jesus's View
In Isaiah 53:3–4 we read prophetically of Jesus:

> He was despised and forsaken of men, a man of sorrows and acquainted with grief; and like one from whom men hide their face He was despised, and we did not esteem Him. Surely our griefs He Himself bore, and our sorrows He carried; yet we ourselves esteemed Him stricken, smitten of God, and afflicted.

Jesus came to redeem everything that robs us of what God created us to be. He came to redeem all of our griefs and sorrows, and since that was His mission in an eternal sense, it is no surprise that He would respond to pain as clearly as He did in the temporal sense.

> As He passed by, He saw a man blind from birth. And His disciples asked Him, "Rabbi, who sinned, this man or his

parents, that he would be born blind?" Jesus answered, "It was neither that this man sinned, nor his parents; but it was so that the works of God might be displayed in him. We must work the works of Him who sent Me as long as it is day; night is coming when no one can work. While I am in the world, I am the Light of the world." When He had said this, He spat on the ground, and made clay of the spittle, and applied the clay to his eyes, and said to him, "Go, wash in the pool of Siloam" (which is translated, Sent). So he went away and washed, and came back seeing. (John 9:1–7)

For a moment, think back to where this story started. Jesus was in the temple debating the religious leaders, and upon His claim to be the "I Am" the enraged crowd picks up stones to execute Him. He disappeared into the temple and escaped the first-century equivalent of a lynching.

As we considered that dangerous scenario, we saw that the King James Version rendered the final verse of John 8, "Jesus hid himself, and went out of the temple, going through the midst of them, and so passed by" (v. 59). That phrase connects directly to John 9:1, because as Jesus passed by He didn't keep passing by! He stopped to consider the need of one man, even though Jesus was at great personal risk—humanly speaking. People were trying to kill Him, but He stops and stands and stays. And helps.

This is the underlying point of the story. Jesus was more concerned with the needs of this man than He was for His own safety. Even more, Jesus was more concerned about the needs of this man than about the religious regulations that seemed so paramount to the religionists.

In John 8:12, Jesus had declared himself to be the "Light of the world," and He reasserts that dramatic claim in John 9:5, "While I am in the world, I am the Light of the world." This claim would be nothing more than an exercise in metaphor (or perhaps even hyperbole) if it were left to just hang in the air. But Jesus doesn't leave it to hang in the air. Instead, by bringing light to the darkness of this man who has never known sight, He moves forcefully and dramatically to prove that He is the Light of the world.

Jesus spits on the ground and makes clay, and then He rubs it in the blind man's eyes. To the casual observer, this would actually seem to make the situation worse—not better. It's bad enough that the man can't see, but even if he somehow could see, his eyes are now blocked by the mud Jesus has made and applied. Why does Jesus do this? The text doesn't tell us, but one writer speculated that since the Creator had made man from the dust of the earth He knew where to find spare parts when the man was broken.

Earlier, when we looked at the disciples' viewpoint, we saw that they were most interested in placing blame for the man's blindness. Much like them, we often deteriorate into a culture of blame. As long as we can attach responsibility to someone else for the wrongs in the world and the pains in our lives, we can feel somehow exonerated. Jesus's concern, however, is not who is to blame for the situation. His concern is to bring solution to the problem by doing what He is claiming to be able to do—bring light to the world. And Jesus did just that.

A Gospel Challenge—Rooted In Perspective

Upon applying the mud to the man's eyes, Jesus instructs him to go wash the mud out of his eyes in the Pool at Siloam. This exchange is connected to what Jesus is trying to communicate to His followers about His mission. His mission was to bring light to a sin-darkened world, and Jesus would accomplish that mission while enduring the darkness of sin-bearing on the cross on our behalf. He would do that because that was why He had been sent by the Father.

The key word here is *sent*. It is intentional and purposeful. It is a missional term that is unambiguous, and it pervades this conversation. Jesus challenges His theologically absorbed disciples to see the big picture (v. 4) by saying, "We must work the works of *Him who sent Me* as long as it is day; night is coming when no one can work" (John 9:4; emphasis added).

Then, Jesus *sent* the man to the Pool of Siloam, which means, well, "sent" (see v. 7). This play on words does not appear to be coincidental. It is Jesus patiently walking His disciples through the most genuine reality in the universe—that the Father sent the Son the be the Savior of the world (1 John 4:14) and that Jesus now sends His followers into that same world to tell the good news that the Savior has arrived. Jesus's first words to His disciples on resurrection day were an extension of this discussion on mission: "So Jesus said to them again, 'Peace be with you; as the Father has *sent* Me, I also *send* you'" (John 20:21; emphasis added).

Our God is a God of rescue and restoration, of help and healing. When we respond to the needs of others, God's glory is revealed to those who are most in need. So, do we see those around us as nonentities, curiosities, sinful, embarrassments—or as objects of the Creator's love who may be drawn to Him if they can see His glory displayed in acts of grace?

Our perspective on the people our God loves will determine the extent to which we will serve the Light of the world, who said: "You are the light of the world. . . . Let your light shine before men in such a way that they may see your good works, and glorify your Father who is in heaven" (Matthew 5:14, 16).

One classic hymn beautifully combines the twin themes of this story—light and sending—with familiar words:

> Send the light, the blessed gospel light;
> Let it shine from shore to shore!
> Send the light, the blessed gospel light;
> Let it shine forevermore!
> —*Charles H. Gabriel, 1890*

A Heart That Challenges
Jesus and Pilate

In 1950s America, I was enthralled—as were most boys of that era—with the television program *Adventures of Superman*. As the opening credits of each episode wound down and the Man of Steel was pictured standing in front of an American flag, I found myself—as a child of the Cold War—thankful that the infant Kal-El (who would become Clark Kent, the mild-mannered reporter whose alter ego was Superman) had landed in America's heartland and not in Soviet Russia. Why? Because Superman was here to do more than merely be super (as if that was not enough). He was here to defend "truth, justice, and the American way." It was comforting to know that *we* had him. We could all sleep peacefully knowing that truth, justice, and the American way were secure. Superman was one of us.

For an impressionable grade-schooler, this imagery was evocative. And most significantly, the idea these images evoked was the implication that those three values—truth, justice, and the American way—had been permanently linked together. Where there was the American way, there was truth and justice. Where there was justice, there was truth and the American way. And so on.

Unfortunately, age and experience teaches us that reality is not even remotely that simple. Our world is far more noted for injustice than for justice, the American way has become a rather obscure idea at best, and truth seems to have become an elusive concept. This, of course, is not a new condition. French philosopher Blaise Pascal (1623–1662) said, "Justice and truth are too such subtle points that our tools are too blunt to touch them accurately."

Pascal had a point about the challenging nature of truth—a point that had been lamented centuries earlier by a career politician who was faced with a moral dilemma. He responded by wondering aloud, "What is truth?" That question has become synonymous with its speaker, Pontius Pilate, and is eternally important for us to understand. This is especially vital when we realize that the unmeasured Answer to Pilate's question was standing right in front of him.

An Unclear Past

The late 1990s film *That Thing You Do* follows the journey of a fictional '60s garage band, The Wonders, as it finds itself on top of the charts and preparing to perform on America's most popular television variety show. As they stand onstage, Lenny, a guitarist, turns to Guy, the drummer, and asks, "How did we get here?"

That is a great question. No event ever occurs in a vacuum. Every event occurs in a context of time and space, as the confluence of circumstances shapes and at times propels the events to often unforeseen results. "How did we get here?" is one of the most instructive questions we can ask when seeking to understand any moment in time—and the same is true with the trials of Christ. The Gospels tell us how Jesus had arrived in the court of Judea's leading Roman official. But how did that Roman official get there?

Who was he? Mystery shrouds the background of Pontius Pilate. His name contains more questions than answers. Pontius may be a reference to the Latin family name Pontii, a family group of Samnites. Pilate (or, *Pilatus* in Latin) has less clarity, with a commonly accepted definition being "one skilled with the javelin." As to his place of birth, two ancient traditions vie for supremacy. The first claims he was from the Samnite village of Bisenti in central Italy. The second is more exotic. In it, Pilate comes from ancient Scotland, where his father (the Roman ambassador) sired him illegitimately with a Pict girl. This allegedly occurred in the Scot village of Fortingall, Perthshire, which contains ruins called "The House of Pilate."

His early career is likewise undefined, but upon his arrival in Judea the fog begins to lift. His rank was that of prefect, with duties involving military leadership, collection of the imperial tax, and serving in a judicial capacity. That he possessed the high rank of prefect speaks of his ascendancy in the Roman political scene. That he practiced that rank in a remote outpost like Judea may speak of his having fallen out of favor with Rome.

If so, that would certainly explain his ruthless responses to at least two major crises with the Jews. These realities could speak of a man who was doubly desperate—desperate to prove his strength as a leader and desperate to avoid another high-profile failure. Those events, described by first-century historians Philo and Josephus, reveal a man who would be rebuked by Tiberius Caesar for provoking a riot by bringing Roman implements (mostly shields) that bore graven images of Caesar into Jerusalem. The Jewish law, of course, forbade graven images (Exodus 20:4). The resulting riot threatened more than the peace—it could have resulted in a massacre of thousands of Jewish protestors and the violence previous Roman prefects had bent over backwards to avoid.

The second incident threw fuel on the fire, as Pilate commandeered funds from the temple in Jerusalem to complete the construction of an aqueduct that would bring much-needed water

from the north country to the southern desert regions. The legit-
imacy of the project was irrelevant to the people. "Holy" money
had been redirected by a pagan ruler for a pagan project. This time,
the incident did result in bloodshed. When the Jewish people pro-
tested, Pilate unleashed his troops—killing dozens of protesters.

"How did we get here?" That, indeed, is a productive question
to ask. In this case, the Pilate who has been challenged by the
Jewish people and confronted by the Jewish leadership will now
find himself cornered by the same adversaries. This time, however,
he faces them knowing that he cannot afford another failure. He
cannot afford another bad report to Caesar. His options in the
present are seriously hamstrung by the consequences of his past
missteps. His actions in the present tense would be predicated on
the result of his choices in the past.

Facing the Challenge

American humorist Will Rogers said, "If you ever injected truth
into politics, you have no politics." While it would be easy (and
even a little fun) to pile on with dozens of such quotes about politics, the reality of the political world is actually pretty simple.
The art of politics is the art of the deal. Negotiations, brokering,
arm-twisting, and favors are all part of the tool kit of the politician
to get the deal done. This is the politician's craft—and it is also
the politician's problem. Getting the deal done is a job that, some
would say, requires saying or doing whatever is necessary to seal
the deal. Often, our strengths become our weaknesses—and the
ability of a career politician to be a dealmaker can also be the very
thing that can insulate him or her from recognizing, embracing,
or valuing truth.

With that, I submit to you Pontius Pilate—career politician.
He is a political official who knew the value of closing the deal

but who lacked the moral fiber to rule according to justice. In the opening act of Jesus's trial before Pilate, the dialogue is between the judge (Pilate) and the accusers—with hardly a notice of the Accused. The deal? Pilate seeks to negotiate a result in the trial of Jesus that will prevent another riot or at least absolve himself of any guilt in it.

- Upon first encountering the religious leaders, Pilate attempts to shed responsibility for the impending execution of Jesus by deferring to his former adversaries and current irritants (John 18:28–31). They are not buying what Pilate is selling. So . . .
- Pilate sends Jesus to Herod, ruler of Galilee (Jesus's home region), so he can deal with (and Pilate can escape) the problem. Herod is delighted at the prospects of being entertained by the miracle worker (Luke 23:5–12) but disappointed by Christ's silence. He also refuses to deal, which would result in sending Jesus back. So . . .
- In a last-ditch effort to escape this dilemma, Pilate cites local rules regarding the Passover, which allowed for the release of a prisoner (Matthew 27:15–21). Thinking he had found an escape route, he offered to release Jesus—but the crowd instead demanded the notorious terrorist Barabbas. So . . .
- Pilate reaffirmed his conclusion of Jesus's innocence but sought to placate the crowd by having Jesus savagely beaten (Luke 23:16). Still, however, the crowd would not make the deal. So . . .
- Ever the pragmatist, Pilate chooses to execute the Innocent in order to preserve the peace for a moment (Matthew 27:24).

Truth and politics is a marriage that should be inviolate, but it tends instead to be an abusive relationship. Pilate, caught in the vise grips of politics and expediency, confronts Christ with the question of the ages:

> Therefore Pilate said to Him, "So You are a king?" Jesus answered, "You say correctly that I am a king. For this I have been born, and for this I have come into the world, to testify to the truth. Everyone who is of the truth hears My voice." Pilate said to Him, "What is truth?" And when he had said this, he went out again to the Jews and said to them, "I find no guilt in Him." (John 18:37–38)

English philosopher Francis Bacon (1561–1625) wrote, "'What is truth?' said jesting Pilate; and would not stay for an answer." Was Pilate really jesting? Was his comment about truth just casual sarcasm? We just don't know.

Here is what *The Bible Knowledge Commentary* says:

> Pilate's question, "What is truth?" has echoed down through the centuries. How his question was intended is problematic. Was it a wistful desire to know what no one could tell him? Was it philosophical cynicism concerning the problem of epistemology? Was it indifference to anything so impractical as abstract thought? Or was it irritation at Jesus' response? These are all possible interpretations of his words. But the significant thing is that he suddenly turned away from the *One* who is "the Truth" (John 14:6) without waiting for an answer.

In the very least, Jesus's answer to this question bewildered Pilate. Jesus asserted that His kingdom was not of this world. As Bible teacher John Gill (1697–1771) put it, "the kingdom itself does not appear in worldly pomp and splendour, nor is it supported by worldly force, nor administered by worldly laws." Jesus did not, however, deny that "king" could be His proper title. He affirmed His kingdom and that it had a different origin and a different character from any Pilate knew.

Then came the final blow—Jesus declared that His purpose was to give testimony to truth, and He intimated that anyone who was devoted to truth would listen to Him. Amazing! Moments away from the cross, Jesus was more interested in appealing to Pilate than He was in defending himself.

This was Jesus's consistent method, for His focus was on reaching the heart of the person He addressed. He made an appeal to Pilate, but it was not an appeal for acquittal or mercy for himself. It is the very essence of His mission, "For this I have been born, and for this I have come into the world" (John 18:37). He had come to seek and to save the lost. But it was not only the beggars and lepers and prostitutes and publicans He had come to save. Christ had also come to save the wealthy, the mighty, and the powerful.

Pilate understood the truth of the situation ("I find no guilt in Him" v. 38) but did not know how to properly weigh the gravitas of his own personal moment of truth. Caught between the Rock of ages and a temporal hard place, Pilate sacrificed Truth on the altar of expediency and looked for a way out. Since no one else was willing to get on board with his strategies, Pilate made the deal with himself—because that is what career politicians do, they deal. But if he thought that the deal would give him relief from the pressure he faced, Pontius Pilate was sadly mistaken.

Contents Under Pressure

Someone has said that life is like the weather—there are times of high pressure and times of low pressure, but there are no times of no pressure. Pilate would have affirmed that notion. His career as prefect (governor, procurator) of Judea had been a pressure-cooker ever since he had arrived in AD 26. Crisis had followed crisis, sometimes because of Pilate and sometimes in spite of him.

Now Jesus stands before him on trial—and the pressure rises again. Pilate has already wilted before the pressure of the religious intelligentsia. He has already buckled under the pressure of the mob. He has already sacrificed any remaining shred of integrity he may have had left in order to maintain the facade of stability in Judea. But as challenging as these external pressures are, there are other, more difficult types of pressure.

There are also the internal pressures that eat at the heart and disturb the mind. These are the pressures that cry out for us to do what is good and right and just—only to be shouted down by our desire for self-preservation or even worse, self-promotion. Woven through the accounts of the trials of Christ, these internal pressures come to the prefect of Judea through three very surprising sources—demanding his undivided attention.

Pressure from Unknown Forces. Interestingly, though John's gospel contains the most detailed account of Pilate's interview with Christ, Matthew's gospel reveals what is the most curious piece of the story—and reveals that there were pressures at work that Pilate could have never deduced. As the trial dragged on, Pilate found himself trapped by the events around him spiraling out of control as a message from his wife arrives in his court. "While he was sitting on the judgment seat, his wife sent him a message, saying, 'Have nothing to do with that righteous Man; for last night I suffered greatly in a dream because of Him'" (Matthew 27:19).

Now *that* is interesting. In the ancient world, much stock was placed in dreams, so this message from Pilate's wife (who is identified by tradition as Procla or Procula) would have deeply shaken his threadbare resolve. He must have wondered—where had these dreams come from, and why had they so disturbed his wife? Are there other forces at play here that I can't see? These questions would pile even more pressure on the procurator of Rome.

His response to this pressure? Not to release Christ but to offer Barabbas in His place—a strategy that would fail miserably.

Pressure from Conscience. Pilate's words, "I find no guilt in Him" are followed by his pleading with the crowd that Jesus should be released (Matthew 27:22–23). When his efforts were again fruitless, he responded—not by letting Jesus go but by having Him scourged (v. 26).

This was not a light response—it was drastic. Jewish law limited a scourging to forty lashes (Deuteronomy 25:2–3), so the Jews lowered it to thirty-nine in order to avoid accidentally violating the law by miscounting the blows. Rome had no such limits. They performed scourgings with a desire to inflict as much pain as possible without so much pain that the sufferer would find the relief of death. If Pilate was trying to satiate the crowd, he would be disappointed. They cried all the more for Jesus's crucifixion.

Pressure from Fear. The greatest fear for Pilate came when the religious leaders admitted to the actual reason for their demands for crucifixion—Jesus claimed to be the Son of God (John 19:7). John's account says that the reality of this claim got Pilate's attention, resulting in these words: "Therefore when Pilate heard this statement, he was even more afraid" (v. 8).

First his wife's dream, then the innocence of the Condemned, then the thought that Jesus might be the Son of God. In fear,

Pilate pursued further answers from Christ—and what he heard from Jesus only added to the pressure he felt:

> Jesus answered, "You would have no authority over Me, unless it had been given you from above; for this reason he who delivered Me to you has the greater sin." As a result of this Pilate made efforts to release Him, but the Jews cried out saying, "If you release this Man, you are no friend of Caesar; everyone who makes himself out to be a king opposes Caesar." Therefore when Pilate heard these words, he brought Jesus out, and sat down on the judgment seat at a place called The Pavement, but in Hebrew, Gabbatha. (John 19:11–13)

The result of all of this pressure?

- Pilate allowed the execution of a Man he had himself declared to be innocent.
- Pilate succumbed to the external pressure to do wrong instead of the internal pressure to do right.
- Pilate attempted to wash his hands of any possible guilt in the matter, but he has been seen to have blood on his hands for two millennia.

Pilate has been marked as a man for whom truth was a mystery—even though he faced Truth directly.

A Striking Reality

As Pilate muddled over the question of what truth is, Truth was standing before Him—being judged largely on the basis of lies. Truth—Jesus—stood trial before Pilate that day.

Why is this so vital? Because the Gospel of John does not see truth conceptually, choosing instead to personalize truth in Jesus Christ. John's gospel account uses the word *truth* more than any other book of the Bible—and it almost exclusively refers to Christ himself. In John's uses of the term *truth*, particularly those that refer directly to Christ, his purpose is clear: truth is not a philosophical concept or an abstract theory. Truth is not defined or determined by the mood of the mob or by the person with the most degrees or the most influence. Truth is Christ. How definitively does John assert this? Here are a few statements (with emphasis added):

- John 1:14: "And the Word became flesh, and dwelt among us, and we saw His glory, glory as of the only begotten from the Father, full of grace and *truth*."
- John 1:17: "For the Law was given through Moses; grace and *truth* were realized through Jesus Christ."
- John 8:32 : "You will know the *truth*, and the *truth* will make you free."
- John 8:40: "You are seeking to kill Me, a man who has told you the *truth*, which I heard from God; this Abraham did not do."
- John 8:45: "Because I speak the *truth*, you do not believe Me."
- John 14:6: Jesus said to him, "I am the way, and the *truth*, and the life; no one comes to the Father but through Me."
- John 17:19: "For their sakes I sanctify Myself, that they themselves also may be sanctified in *truth*."

In each case, John is (often quoting Christ) using *truth* as a metaphor for Christ and/or His mission. Why? Because Christ came "full of grace and truth" (John 1:14) to put truth on display for the world to see and respond to. He demonstrated the truth about His own identity, the truth about the Father, the truth about our need, and the truth about His mission. No wonder He—the One who had told them the truth (John 8:40)—was executed by the established powers of His generation.

George Orwell said, "In times of universal deceit, telling the truth will be a revolutionary act." To most of our world, revolutions must be stopped—even the revolutionary truth of eternal life through the One who is the Truth. Pilate's washed hands did not end his troubles. History says Pilate was called back to Rome, with one ancient account saying that his life ended as a suicide. A life built on political machinations inevitably was caught in the gears of the political machine and ground to bits.

The few extrabiblical historical references to Pilate describe him as a petty bureaucrat of bad temper and stubborn spirit, but as the *New Bible Dictionary* says, "The verdict of the [New Testament] is that he was a weak man, ready to serve expediency rather than principle." Pilate faced the Truth—and turned away. In the truest, most eternal sense, Pilate could not handle the Truth.

Embracing the Challenge

A pivotal person in American history was a woman named Isabella Baumfree. Admittedly, most Americans do not recognize that name, yet this woman was a crucial player in some of the earliest moments of moral crisis in the American experiment. Born a slave in about 1797, Isabella was able to escape with her daughter in 1826. Then she went to court to regain possession of her son. In so doing, she became the first African-American woman to win a case of that nature against a white slave owner. She would go on to become one of the leaders of the American abolitionist movement and an early leader of the fight for women's rights.

One could ask, "If she has accomplished all of that, why haven't we heard of her?" Well, we have—but by a different name. In 1843, Isabella Baumfree changed her name to Sojourner Truth— and that name became the description of her life-journey from then until her death in 1883. Her life was dramatically marked by a pursuit of truth that would also champion justice and in a sense redefine the American way. Why? Because truth was *worth* pursuing, and she answered the challenge to pursue it. The truth of her generation was that the American way could never truly reach the highest pinnacle of its potential as long as it was allowed to oppress and dehumanize its own citizens (whether they had the rights of citizenship or not). In the realm of human rights, Sojourner Truth believed and practiced the words of Christ, "You shall know the truth, and the truth shall set you free."

But that reality was not to be restricted to the realm of sociology or government. The truth that marked Isabella Baumfree's crusade in the public arena is even more acutely a fact in the most private of arenas—the human heart. Jesus challenged Pilate to see and embrace truth. And Pilate's failure to respond reminds us that this same challenge awaits each of us. What is truth, and where can we find it?

That is why John's record of the words of the Savior is so critical. In the upper room, hours before embracing the cross that would rescue human beings from the necessary consequences of their sin, Jesus said: "I am the way, and the truth, and the life; no one comes to the Father but through Me" (John 14:6).

Once again, the lesson was profoundly clear—the issues of way, truth, and life are not conceptual; they are personalized in Christ himself. He is not merely a truth-speaker; He is truth itself. He is the truth that sets us free—because He himself is the truth that makes a way for us to the Father and secures for us the promise of life. "What is truth?" is, in a sense, the wrong question. The better question is, "Who is truth?" And the eternal Answer is Jesus Christ.

A Final Word

If nothing else, this book has been an exploration of why the Gospels are good news.

- They are good news because we see Christ in action, responding to the needs of hurting people.
- They are good news because the Father's heart is made visible in Jesus's tangible acts of care and concern.
- They are good news because each event moves Jesus ever closer to the cross and His ultimate act of concern for our deepest, most enduring needs.

In the Gospels, we come face-to-face with our Creator and observe as He takes us in hand to repair the brokenness that was never His creative intent for those who bear His image. We see Him working to move people in the direction of the Father—and the purpose for which they had been created.

Vaclav Havel, the first president of the Czech Republic, wrote, "The tragedy of modern man is not that he knows less and less about the meaning of his own life, but that it bothers him less and less." In these chapters, I have been bothered. Bothered about where I personally might see my own place in these stories. Bothered by the extent of work the Savior has to do to help me live out His purposes. Bothered that I'm not more bothered by my shortcomings and failings. Bothered.

But may I suggest that this is actually a good thing? Being bothered by where we are is the first step to letting Him walk with us to where He knows we need to be. So to that end I encourage you to join me in reflecting on one of the great benedictions in the Scriptures:

> Now the God of peace, who brought up from the dead the great Shepherd of the sheep through the blood of the eternal covenant, even Jesus our Lord, equip you in every good thing to do His will, working in us that which is pleasing in His sight, through Jesus Christ, to whom be the glory forever and ever. Amen. (Hebrews 13:20–21)

This is the root of our hope, and the good news of the Gospels—He came to get us there. To wholeness and rightness and usefulness. To get us to the point where we please the Father. To get us to where we were created to be. The good news is that Jesus, who worked in the lives of the men and women we have considered in this book, is actively working in us today. Actively pulling us to Him. Actively making us what we were always supposed to be.

In the midst of a world filled with bad news, yes, this is good news. This is gospel. Because this is why Jesus came. For you and for me.

Reflection Questions

Chapter One: A Heart That Touches

- In today's world what might parallel the plight of the leper? What makes that parallel work?
- Which is more shocking to you, the boldness of the leper or the welcome he received from Jesus?
- What do you make of the disobedience of the healed leper? In your mind is it understandable, or is it unforgiveable?
- How might you seek to live out the heart Jesus displayed to this leper for the outcasts of our generation?

Chapter Two: A Heart That Marvels

- Have you or someone you loved served in the military? What makes the life of a soldier so difficult? What might make it rewarding?
- Which surprises you more about the centurion, his love for conquered Israel or his concern for his servant boy? Why?
- The elders of the synagogue offer a strong appeal to Jesus to answer the centurion's request. Which surprises you more, that they would intervene on behalf of a pagan Roman or that they clearly believe Jesus is capable of healing the boy? Why?
- How do you handle the fact that Jesus marveled at the centurion's faith? Does this speak to Jesus's humanity, the depth of the centurion's faith, or the lack of faith in Israel? Why?

Chapter Three: A Heart That Accepts

- Social taboos exist in every culture. What are some social taboos in your culture that you respect? That you find annoying? In each case, why?
- This is one of several times we will see Jesus help someone who is not one of the lost sheep of the house of Israel. Search for the word "Samaritan" in the Gospels. How is it used negatively, and how is it seen positively? In each case, who is using the term "Samaritan" in that way?
- What do you think the disciples would have found more shocking—that Jesus was talking with a Samaritan, or that this Samaritan was a woman? What does this interaction say about Jesus's heart for the needs of this woman?
- We often bend to social taboos rather than cause a problem in the community. How could you learn to value people more than you value those traditions—without being disrespectful to tradition?

Chapter Four: A Heart That Cares

- In your experience, do you see respect and opportunities for women growing or declining? Why?
- In Jesus's culture (and Roman culture), women were lightly valued. How did Jesus's actions fly in the face of those cultural tendencies?
- In dealing with the woman, Jesus called her out in front of the crowd—dealing with her very publicly. How does that hit you? Why might it have been appropriate?
- In the dealing with the little girl, Jesus isolated her from the crowd—dealing with her privately. How does that hit you? Why might that have been appropriate?

Chapter Five: A Heart That Confronts

- Have you ever been on the receiving end of religious arrogance or judgmental treatment? How did that feel? How has that influenced your thinking about religion in general and religious people in particular?
- In failing to show common hospitality to Jesus, what unspoken message was Simon communicating about his honored guest?
- How do you view the woman's hubris in barging into this scene? How were her actions a compensation for Simon's lack of hospitality?
- One of the takeaways of this episode is that we look on the outward appearance and God sees the heart. How might you become more intentional about looking beyond the outward appearance when dealing with others?

Chapter Six: A Heart That Reaches

- Do you like puzzles? After reading about this encounter, can you see why one writer called it "the most puzzling event in Jesus's ministry"?
- Which was more troubling to you in the initial encounter with the woman—Jesus's silence or the disciples' obvious animosity toward her? Why?
- What are some indications that Jesus was conveying nonverbal signals to the woman? How do her responses reinforce this idea?
- We saw in this episode that not everything that happens *to* us is *for* us. Sometimes our struggles are to benefit others. When have you experienced benefit from someone else's difficulties? When has someone else benefitted from your struggles?

Chapter Seven: A Heart That Restores

- Why does blindness form such an appropriate metaphor for those without Christ? How does Jesus's dealings with the various New Testament blind men reinforce this metaphor?

- In this event, Jesus uses a methodology that differs from His dealing with other blind men. Why is that significant, and how does it show how personally Jesus loves and cares for individuals?

- What do you make of the two cycles of ministry that Mark records? How do the two healings (deaf man, blind man)—both unique to Mark—contribute to Mark's preparation for the events of Caesarea Philippi?

- With whom do you most resonate in this story—the friends of the blind man, the blind man, or the disciples? Why?

Chapter Eight: A Heart That Comforts

- The imagery of mountaintop experiences and life in the valley has vivid connotations. What most speaks to your own experience—the mountaintop or the valley? Why?

- The contrast between the Father and Son on the mountain and the father and son in the valley could not be more stark. Which do you feel more deeply—the glory of the Son or the agony of the father?

- How did the failure of the disciples reflect on them? How did it reflect on Jesus?

- One of the most honest statements in the Bible is the phrase, "I believe, help my unbelief." In what ways have you experienced that tension in your own relationship with God?

Chapter Nine: A Heart That Transforms

- How do you respond to the tension of living in such a polarized world? Retreat? Take a stand? Deflect?

- Prejudice can take many forms—racial, socio-economic, political. Have you ever been on the receiving end of such prejudice, and if so, what was the cause of the prejudice and what was it like?
- Jesus was constantly violating the taboos of His generation. How might the fact that Jesus had included a tax collector among His closest disciples have been an encouragement to Zaccheus? How did Jesus's self-invitation to dinner at Zaccheus's home reinforce His love and concern for the marginalized?
- How could you work, by His Spirit, to deal with any tendencies toward prejudice in your own heart?

Chapter Ten: A Heart That Forgives

- Have you ever felt as if you were being used or manipulated? What was that like? Were there consequences that flowed from that experience?
- It is amazing the degree to which the religious leaders were able to pick and choose what they would apply and what they would ignore in order to accomplish their goals. But is the end worth the means if the means is a surrender of biblical and personal integrity? Why or why not?
- While we cannot know the truth of what Jesus wrote in the dirt, it clearly had an impact on the religious leaders calling for the woman's execution. Is it significant to you that they left "beginning with the oldest"? What might that indicate?
- Given the fact that Jesus showed care for the woman rather than using her (like the religious leaders), how can we be more intentional about loving rather than using others?

Chapter Eleven: A Heart That Values

- In the illustration of the elephant and the blind men, we learn the value of perspective. How can we more wisely factor perspective into the judgments and decisions we make? How might counsel from others help in broadening our perspective?

- Which of the perspectives about the blind man do you find most understandable? Most disturbing? In each case, why?

- Which is more unsettling, the persistent unbelief of the religionists or the parents' inability to celebrate their son's sight? What can you learn from each perspective?

- How we view others may be very different from how God views them. Ask Him to help you to have a perspective that shows compassion for others.

Chapter Twelve: A Heart That Challenges

- What is your overall perspective on politics in today's world? Is it positive or negative? Why?

- Many times in film adaptations of Jesus's trial, Pilate is portrayed somewhat sympathetically. Do you find him a sympathetic character? Why or why not?

- Can you identify with the pressures Pilate felt? Do you enjoy pressurized situations (some people do!), or do you seek to avoid them?

- In a generation of relativism, how do you see the value of truth (or lack of value)? How does that affect your view of Jesus—the Truth?

Enjoy this book? Help us get the word out!

Share a link to the book or
mention it on social media

Write a review on your blog, on a retailer site,
or on our website (dhp.org)

Pick up another copy to share with someone

Recommend this book for your
church, book club, or small group

Follow Discovery House on
social media and join the discussion

Contact us to share your thoughts:

 @discoveryhouse    @DiscoveryHouse

Discovery House
P.O. Box 3566
Grand Rapids, MI 49501 USA

Phone: 1-800-653-8333
Email: books@dhp.org
Web: dhp.org